THE FUTURE OF FOOD

THE FUTURE OF FOOD

How to Feed the Planet Without
Destroying It

Matt Reynolds

1 3 5 7 9 10 8 6 4 2

Random House Business
20 Vauxhall Bridge Road
London SW1V 2SA

Random House Business is part of the Penguin Random House
group of companies whose addresses can be found at
global.penguinrandomhouse.com.

Penguin
Random House
UK

First published by Random House Business in 2021

www.penguin.co.uk

A CIP catalogue record for this book is available from
the British Library.

ISBN 9781847943286

Typeset in 9.5/18 pt Exchange Text
by Integra Software Services Pvt. Ltd, Pondicherry

Printed and bound in Great Britain by Clays Ltd, Elcograf S.p.A.

The authorised representative in the EEA is Penguin Random House
Ireland, Morrison Chambers, 32 Nassau Street, Dublin D02 YH68.

Penguin Random House is committed to a sustainable future for
our business, our readers and our planet. This book is made from
Forest Stewardship Council® certified paper.

Contents

Introduction: A planet at a crossroads

In May 1968 a Stanford University professor published a book warning that the world was spiralling towards irredeemable disaster. 'The battle to feed all of humanity is over,' read the opening line of *The Population Bomb*, followed by a prediction that the next two decades would be blighted by global famines that would lead to the deaths of hundreds of millions of people. Before its publication the book's author, Paul Ehrlich, was barely known outside the narrow world of entomology, where he was lauded for his studies detailing how butterflies evolved alongside flowering plants. The publication of *The Population Bomb* – co-written with his wife Anne, who remained uncredited on its cover – would turn its author into one of the most prominent doomsayers of the time.

At its heart, Ehrlich's thesis was seductively simple: more people were being added to the planet than could possibly be fed, and so the only solution was to limit the number of people being born. It was an argument that went all the way back to the eighteenth-century economist Thomas Robert Malthus, but Ehrlich's paperback married these ancient fears about planetary overcrowding with growing environmental concerns. Aided by its author's relentless promotion, *The Population Bomb* was a break-out hit. Ehrlich became a frequent guest on the US talk show *The Tonight Show,* where he would discuss the book's advocacy of birth control and mass sterilisation with the show's host, Johnny Carson, in front of an audience of millions. His appearances pushed the book up best-seller charts and it would eventually be reprinted more than 19 times. For Ehrlich, there was no question that humanity was headed towards disaster. It was simply a question of how soon.

There was just one problem. Ehrlich's predictions would prove to be completely incorrect. Rather than stalling, food production in the second half of the twentieth century increased dramatically – propelled upwards by the development of high-tech versions of ancient crops, new tractors and farm machinery, improved irrigation and the increased use of fertilisers. In 1961 an average field of wheat produced 1.09 tonnes of crop per hectare. By 2000 that same hypothetical plot of land was producing two-and-a-half times as much food. In Latin America and India – parts of the world that Ehrlich predicted would be decimated by famine – the increases were even more dramatic. Between 1961 and 2000 in India the yields per hectare of wheat and cassava more than tripled, while those of potatoes, barley and bananas more than doubled. In Mexico, potato and barley yields tripled per hectare, while wheat, corn and banana yields doubled.[1]

All the while the world's population – as Ehrlich feared – kept shooting upwards. In 1960 there were 3.03 billion humans on the planet. By 2000 that number had more than doubled to 6.14 billion.[2] Yet food production wasn't just keeping up with population growth – it was outstripping it. Devastating hunger was still a grim reality – in the 1970s and 1980s an estimated 5.4 million people died due to famine – but the overall trend was the opposite of what Ehrlich predicted. Today, fewer people are dying of famine than at almost any other point in human history, an achievement that Alex de Waal, executive director of the World Peace Foundation, has called a 'huge but unheralded achievement of our era'.[3] In 1970, the year that Ehrlich sat opposite Johnny Carson before a prime-time audience and insisted that the only answer to the world's dilemma was a drastic regime of population control, one in four people in the world went hungry.[4] In 2019 that figure was less than one in ten. Human ingenuity has opened the doors to a new era of abundance, allowing us to skip past Malthus's trap and unlock the planet's potential to feed billions.

This abundance, however, has come with its own set of problems. As fields have become more productive and countries wealthier, so the environmental footprints of our diets have ballooned to staggering proportions. Half of all Earth's habitable land is now used for agriculture, putting at least 28,780 species at risk of extinction, according to data from the International Union for Conservation of Nature. Land isn't the only resource that agriculture is gobbling up: 70 per cent of freshwater drawn from aquifers, streams and lakes goes into agriculture.[5] That freshwater, in turn, is polluted by agricultural chemicals that leak from the land back into the environment. In the summer of 2014, for example, excess fertiliser running from fields into Lake Erie fed toxic blooms of algae that turned the water a bright blue-green and forced nearly half a million people in Toledo, Ohio, to stop using their tap water for drinking, cooking or bathing. Even more dangerous is the impact we can't see: on its own, food production is now responsible for 26 per cent of all human-caused greenhouse-gas emissions. At the same time agriculture is also one of the biggest victims of the climate crisis. In Bangladesh hectares of once-thriving rice paddies are being abandoned as salty water from rising seas makes its way into river deltas, dehydrating and killing crops. The climate crisis is, at its most fundamental level, a crisis in how we produce food. We cannot tackle the challenge of climate change without reducing the impact that our food has on the planet.

Although his direst predictions never came true, Ehrlich was right about one thing: the demand for food is continuing to go up. The population growth rate has slowed since the late 1960s, but by 2050 there will be around 9.7 billion humans on the planet – about two billion more than there are today – according to projections by the United Nations.[6] And the world isn't just getting more populous, it's also getting wealthier and therefore greedier. As GDP (gross domestic product) per capita grows – particularly in the developing world, where most future population growth will be concentrated – the demand for more environmentally impactful food such as beef and dairy is set to go up. In China between 1961 and 2019 meat production increased by more than 3,000 per cent, while per-capita meat consumption went up 15-fold. This double-whammy of population growth and changing demographics is why in 2009 the Food and Agriculture Organization of the United Nations (FAO) estimated that food production will need to increase 70 per cent by 2050, requiring an additional 900 million tonnes of cereal crops and 200 million tonnes of meat every year.[7]

This is the central dilemma facing the planet today: how can we feed billions more people while simultaneously using fewer resources and emitting fewer greenhouse gases? Some look back to the dramatic increases in farm yields in the second half of the twentieth century and see a template there for the future of our food system. Technology helped solve the productivity problem – what if we directed those same energies towards the challenge facing the world today? In Silicon Valley, start-ups are growing meat that has never seen the inside of an animal, with the aim of sidestepping the huge carbon footprint that comes from growing crops to feed livestock. In greenhouses in the Philippines and the UK, researchers are experimenting with creating new crop varieties resistant to drought, salt or disease, which could grow in a world altered by climate change.

Others argue that the solution can't just involve producing more – it will require using *less*. Farming start-ups are hoping that ultra-precise robots can help reduce the amount of herbicide and fertiliser applied to fields, while people in the fish-farming industry are trying to find new ways of feeding fish that don't deplete our oceans even further. Farmers across the globe are already returning to forms of agriculture that rely less on artificial fertilisers and herbicides, in favour of systems that cycle nutrients from crops back into the soil.

But technology alone can only get us so far. It is not simply the way we produce food that needs fixing, but the very system of food production and distribution itself. Right now, the world produces enough food to feed everyone on Earth – yet 746 million people are still severely food-insecure, a figure that is projected to go up in the wake of the Covid-19 pandemic.[8] And while those people go hungry, one-third of food produced for human consumption is lost or wasted globally – around 1.3 billion tonnes of food each year produced in vain.[9] Part of the responsibility for fixing the food crisis also lies with each of us, the decisions we make about what we eat and how much we waste.

Fixing farming. Changing our diets. Reducing waste. These are the challenges the world must overcome in order to feed 9.7 billion by 2050. In the late 1960s thinkers like Paul Ehrlich grasped for a single fix that would wrench the planet out of its bind. Half a century later we know it's possible to grow enough food to feed the planet, but we haven't yet worked out how to produce this food without tipping out of balance the precarious ecological systems that we rely on. Now thousands of farmers, scientists and activists are racing to answer a single question: how can we produce more while using less? At stake is not just the future of food, but the future of our planet.

1

Replacing meat

Mark Post had run out of money. For two years the professor at Eindhoven University of Technology in the Netherlands had been relentlessly trying to coax pig cells into becoming something more than a microscopic blob at the bottom of a Petri dish. It was not a job that he had initially signed up for. A vascular biologist by training, Post was interested mainly in angiogenesis – growing blood vessels in the hope of replacing faulty arteries. The pig cells that Post was working with, however, had nothing to do with repairing damaged hearts. His team was trying to nudge the cells into forming minuscule strips of muscle fibre – a tiny, unappetising pork steak grown entirely outside the animal's body. By 2010 – two years after he inherited the project from a colleague – Post was wondering whether his miniature steaks could be the first step towards solving a much bigger challenge: reversing the huge environmental toll that eating meat takes on the planet.

Finding out if he was right, however, would require more money. A lot more. Growing tissue in a lab is a painstaking, unforgiving process. Once extracted from a living or recently deceased donor animal, cells must be bathed in an eye-wateringly expensive solution usually derived from the blood of cow foetuses, which contains the amino acids, sugars and growth factors that cells need to grow. Feed them enough of this solution, while keeping them at the right temperature and away from any possible contaminants, and the cells will start to divide. Once they have divided enough times, they can be placed on tiny structures that help them grow into muscle tissue. But cells are notoriously fickle. Sometimes they might refuse to turn from their initial state into muscle cells. At other times they stop growing altogether. Post had already burned through his share of a €2 million (£1.7 million) grant that the Dutch government had split between three universities to pursue the project, but his next move would require many, many more muscle fibres than anyone had previously attempted to grow. The professor wanted to grow a pork sausage in his lab, then cook it in front of a public audience while the porcine cell donor ran around onstage in front of him – living proof that humans could still enjoy meat without the staggering inefficiencies that come from rearing an entire animal just to eat a slice of its flesh. But in 2010, with his funding dried up, Post had no way to make that happen.

Meat without animals

The environmental footprint of meat dwarfs that of almost any other foodstuff. In 2018 two environmental scientists – Joseph Poore and Thomas Nemecek – calculated how much pressure our diets exert on the planet.[1] Their dataset covered more than 38,000 farms producing 40 different foodstuffs and measured how food production impacted on the environment in various ways. What they found was a food system where the environmental costs skew dramatically towards meat production. Farming livestock accounts for 77 per cent of all global farming land, even though that livestock ends up providing just 18 per cent of the world's calories and 37 per cent of its total protein. Together, livestock and fisheries account for almost one-third of all greenhouse-gas emissions from farming and for 14.5 per cent of all human-induced greenhouse-gas emissions.[2]

Stack meat up against any non-animal source of protein and you tend to find that the emissions required to take an animal all the way from an embryo to a juicy cut of meat are many times higher. Producing 100 grams of beef protein produces a median of 30 kilograms of carbon-dioxide equivalents.[3] Lamb weighs in at 20 kilograms of carbon-dioxide equivalents, while pork is at 6.5 kilograms. At the opposite end of the scale you have plant-based proteins. Tofu produces just 1.6 kilograms of carbon-dioxide equivalents for every 100 grams of protein. Meanwhile beans weigh in at 0.65 kilograms, thanks to bacteria that lurk in the roots of leguminous plants and provide them with nitrogen, reducing their reliance on artificial fertilisers.

Why does meat have such a large carbon footprint? It's all a question of inputs. In tracking the emissions of those 40 different foods, Poore and Nemecek were totting up all the resources that went into producing and distributing each item. Take soybean as an example. Producing this protein-rich legume requires land that must be made suitable for growing, then fertiliser to nourish the crop, tractors and machinery to maintain and harvest it, and ships and trucks to get the processed product to the end-user. Each of these steps comes with its own carbon cost. With livestock, however, these costs are multiplied. Not only does a pig or chicken farm produce its own emissions from heating, manure and land use, but you also have to count all the emissions that come from feeding those animals. In the US alone, 70 per cent of soybean production goes into animal feed – the majority of it for poultry.

One way of thinking about livestock is as concentrators of protein. They eat vast amounts of plant protein and condense it down into delicious hunks of meat. The problem is that not all of that food goes into the bits of animals that humans enjoy eating. A large chunk of it goes into forming bones, beaks and feathers, is expelled as manure or lost as heat energy. The higher up the food chain we eat, the more these inefficiencies get piled on top of each other, releasing precious carbon emissions into the atmosphere for nothing in return.

When it comes to piling up emissions, cattle farming is the worst culprit. One problem is that cattle are particularly inefficient when it comes to turning feed into body weight. Thanks to their fibre-packed diets and higher energy demands, it takes around six kilograms of feed to produce one kilogram of cow.[4] The other problem with cattle is the methane that they burp up as a consequence of their slow ruminant digestion.

Unfortunately for the planet (and our diets), methane is a potent greenhouse gas, producing 28 times the warming potential of carbon dioxide, and it's the main reason why beef and dairy production has such a high emissions footprint, accounting for 41 and 20 per cent respectively of all emissions from livestock.

Growing meat in a laboratory – or eventually full-sized meat factories – would mean producers could sidestep the methane problem and pour all their resources into making only the parts of animals that people eat: growing ground beef, bacon or chicken breast that never had to squander energy by producing waste or running around a farm.

In the spring of 2010 Mark Post got the call that would solve his cashflow issue and eventually make his name synonymous with the world of cultivated meat. The message was from the office of Sergey Brin, the Russian-American computer scientist who in 1998 co-founded Google with Larry Page and later started funnelling part of his vast wealth into a foundation focused on solving global problems. '[They said] "Well, Sergey would be interested in funding this". I had no idea who Sergey was because they only said their first name, and I thought they said it with such authority that I should probably know who this guy was, but I didn't,' Post says. Brin just had one condition: ditch the sausage and focus on making the world's first cultivated hamburger instead.

The decision to switch to hamburgers was a shrewd one. Not only does beef have the highest greenhouse-gas emissions, but ground beef is also the most popular form of the meat in the US, making up an estimated 60 per cent of all beef sales.[5] Growing a hamburger also made sense from a scientific perspective – although Post's team knew how to grow muscle cells, getting them to form a structure that resembled a cut of meat was much more difficult. By sticking with processed meat, Post wouldn't have to worry so much about the texture of his meat paling in comparison to the real thing. Now armed with the money from Silicon Valley, Post's researchers started racing to nearby slaughterhouses to get muscle samples to grow their hamburger from. 'It has to be fresh. So you really have to go with your Petri dish to the slaughterhouse and ask the slaughterer to take a piece of meat and give it to you – and then you can rush back to the lab,' Post says.

After two years of working on the project Post managed to grow three burgers, each one costing €250,000 (£216,000) – with roughly half the cost accounted for by the materials needed to grow the cells, and the other half taken up by labour. 'Making those hamburgers in an academic lab was a very painful experience. The people were not really trained to do that, they're actually trained to solve scientific problems,' he says. Each 100-gram hamburger contained 10,000 muscle fibres that had to be painstakingly grown from a tiny initial sample of cells weighing just five grams. During the final stretch of production, a stray microbe infected a growing culture, rendering the cells useless and delaying the whole project. Then in August 2013, in a studio on the banks of the River Thames in London, one of the three burgers was cooked by a chef and eaten by the food scientist Hanni

Rützler and journalist Josh Schonwald. (A backup burger went on a brief tour of press conferences with Post, before being preserved in plastic and donated to the Boerhaave Museum in Leiden.) Served on a plate next to three slices of tomato, a salad leaf and a sad-looking bun, the burger contained breadcrumbs and a little salt, but no fat at all and, according to Schonwald, had the taste of an 'animal protein cake'. But the taste and texture were secondary, with this burger. Post had shown the world that it was possible to grow meat that didn't require rearing and killing animals.

The real challenge, however, would be convincing people to actually eat it. Bruce Friedrich has spent decades trying to persuade people to give up eating meat. In his 14 years of working for the animal-rights organisation People for the Ethical Treatment of Animals (PETA), he became known for leading high-profile campaigns that drew crowds of protestors to fast-food chains rechristened 'Kentucky Fried Cruelty', 'Wicked Wendy's' and 'Murder King'. In February 2000 he was arrested after splashing red paint over attendees at New York Fashion Week.[6] A year later he ran in front of Buckingham Palace wearing nothing but a pair of tennis shoes and with the website 'GoVeg.com' painted across his body. When he joined PETA in 1996 Friedrich was convinced that the problem of eating meat – with all its disastrous consequences for animal welfare, the environment and antibiotic resistance – could be solved if he simply got the word out to enough people.[7] 'I thought basically all we have to do is: all the current vegans need to turn one more person vegan in the next five years and we'll have doubled veganism. And then in the next five years, those however-many-vegans double veganism and the vegan multiplier gets us to a vegan world in about sixty years.'

But by 2009 Friedrich was becoming frustrated that this vegan wave wasn't materialising. In fact, the opposite was true. Globally, per-capita meat consumption has steadily risen for the last 60 years. During his tenure at PETA it went up by nearly 20 per cent to 41.5 kilograms per person per year.[8] By weight, there are now more than ten times more animals kept as livestock than there are wild mammals on the planet – each year an estimated 50 billion chickens alone are slaughtered for food.[9] Friedrich had had some successes – generating headlines and getting fast-food chains to improve their welfare standards – but globally he was losing the battle against meat, badly. 'Animal-rights activists and environmental activists and global health people have been begging people to eat less meat. And yet per-capita meat consumption keeps going up and up. There's something about human beings that [means] we want to eat meat,' says Friedrich.

The conclusion he came to was that anti-meat campaigns were doomed to failure. So instead of persuading people to give up meat, Friedrich decided that they needed a better alternative. In 2016 he founded the Good Food Institute (GFI), a Washington DC-based non-profit that is now a linchpin of the new world of cultivated and plant-based meat – funding scientific research into alternative protein and helping start-ups develop in the space. Once one of the meat industry's biggest antagonists, Friedrich now wants to help it transform to an entirely new way of working. In 2016 he drew the ire of animal-rights advocates after penning a *Wall Street Journal* op-ed praising the US meat giant Tyson Foods for investing in the plant-based start-up Beyond Meat. Three years later Tyson Foods would launch a plant-based brand of its own.

In the eight years since Mark Post debuted his quarter-million-euro hamburger, the world of lab-grown meat has exploded from a scientific backwater to a burgeoning start-up scene. In 2016 Post founded a company called Mosa Meat to commercialise lab-grown meat. As of December 2019 there were 40 companies vying to bring cultivated meat or seafood to the market, and the list of animals that have had their flesh recreated in the lab now includes chicken, tuna, pig, duck and kangaroo.[10] In December 2020, Singapore Food Agency approved a cultivated chicken product from the US-based company Eat Just. Diners can now order cultivated meat from a restaurant menu for the first time ever. For Friedrich, the challenge facing the industry is simple: find a way to make products that taste as good as traditional meat while costing the same or less. 'Our market is everybody who eats meat,' he says. 'We want steak, we want ribs, we want fully formed chicken breasts.'

The person with the best chance of making Friedrich's vision of the future of meat a reality may well be Uma Valeti, CEO of the cultivated-meat firm Upside Foods, which changed its name from Memphis Meats in May 2021. A former cardiologist, in 2015 Valeti co-founded Upside Foods with stem-cell biologist Nicholas Genovese. The company has already raised more than $200 million (£137 million) in funding. In the world of cultivated-meat start-ups – where product launches, like funding rounds, are always just around the corner – it can be hard to gauge which companies stand the best chance of going the distance. But Upside Foods is unusual in that its backers include two of the biggest meat producers in the United States, Tyson Foods and Cargill, as well as Bill Gates, Richard Branson and Japanese investment giant SoftBank. Since unveiling the first cultivated meatball in January 2016, Upside Foods has held more than 1,000 small-scale tastings for its lab-grown meats. The challenge for Valeti is finding a way to drive the cost of the product down. Like Friedrich, he knows that unless it can compete with conventional meat producers on price, cultivated meat won't have a hope of making a dent in the United States' trillion-dollar meat industry. 'We know we can do multiple species. We can do land and avian and marine, but we need to be able to do that at a cost that would be scalable and would make the difference we are looking for,' he says.

In the last five years the cost of growing meat in a lab has come down dramatically. Upside Foods' first meatball cost $39,600 (£28,000) per kilogram, but by March 2017, when the company held a public tasting of cultivated duck and chicken, the cost had fallen to $5,280 (£4,200) per kilogram. Much of this has been driven by reductions in the cost of cell-culture media, the nutrient-rich soup that cells are bathed in while they grow and develop. Most cell-culture media is intended for use in university laboratories or biomedical research centres, which typically require much smaller volumes than the cultivated-meat industry needs to grow meat at scale – a 3,500-kilogram batch of meat could require anything between 20,000 and 140,000 litres of culture media, costing an estimated $377 (£288) per litre.[11] One study from the Good Food Institute estimates that this media accounts for between 55 and 95 per cent of the marginal cost of growing meat, once you take fixed costs like buildings and equipment out of the equation. Krijn De Nood, CEO of a Dutch cultivated-meat start-up called Meatable, confirmed that media costs were at the higher end of that range. If firms can crack the media problem, the cost of meat will come tumbling down. It is little wonder, then, that cultivated-meat start-ups closely guard the exact ingredients of their nutrient broths, although Upside Foods, Mosa Meat and Meatable have all developed cell-feed formulations that are free from animal-derived serum – a sticking point for an industry that exists to reduce our reliance on slaughtering animals for food. According to Valeti, Upside Foods has already seen a 90 per cent reduction in the cost of media since 2017, and finding ways to make cells better at turning their food into growth will help reduce costs even further. It's progress, but still a long way off a half-kilogram packet of premium ground beef, which would cost a New Yorker a little under eight dollars from a Manhattan Whole Foods. 'That's been our journey the last few years, just bringing the price to a point where we feel premium producers and premium consumers would be able to buy it if we set up a pilot plant,' says Valeti.

Not far from the start-up's headquarters in Berkeley, California, Upside Foods has already broken ground on a pilot production facility – one of the first of its kind anywhere in the world. Valeti demurs over the precise details of the meat factory (how much meat it will be able to produce, or what kind), but at its core will be a series of bioreactors where cells grow and divide before they are seeded onto scaffolds and encouraged to mature into the cells that make up meat: fat, muscle cells and connective tissue. To an outside observer, the plant will look a little like a brewery, but instead of beer, the rows of bioreactors will be brewing up meat. Aside from the cells themselves and the media used to help them grow, these bioreactors (Valeti prefers the term 'cultivators') are the most important part of the cultivated-meat puzzle – they are what will take lab-grown meat from the world of small-scale experimentation to the dream of fully functioning meat factories.

Bioreactors are critical because cells are extremely fickle. 'They're used to being in a body that is very precisely temperature-controlled,' says Liz Specht, associate director of science and technology at the Good Food Institute. Bioreactors act as surrogate bodies for cells grown outside animals. They help regulate temperature, take away waste, provide the right flow of nutrients and make sure oxygen and acidity levels stay within the narrow window cells require for survival. As bioreactors get bigger, balancing all of these requirements becomes more difficult, while the risks of failure dramatically increase. Specht estimates that most start-ups are still working with bioreactors that hold between 50 and 200 litres of media – enough to grow roughly a kilogram of meat. If a pump gets clogged or a thermometer goes haywire in a small bioreactor, it might ruin the day of the technician working on it, but it's unlikely to be too much of a setback. If a 20,000-litre bioreactor goes wrong, by contrast, you've got a disaster on your hands – potentially millions of dollars of meat wasted. 'I think the biggest scientific challenge will be around the engineering of how do you scale up that tissue bioreactor design? How do you automate that process?' says Specht.

Billions of years of evolution have made mammalian bodies masters at distributing the ingredients of life – oxygen and nutrients – to where they are needed. In the human body, almost every single cell is within 200 micrometres of a blood vessel: no more than the width of two human hairs placed side by side. Any further than that and the cell can't access the nutrients it needs to survive. This poses a conundrum for start-ups growing meat in bioreactors, and particularly those that want to recreate cuts of meat that have more complicated structures, such as steak, ribs or chicken breast. How can they make sure that every cell has access to the nutrients it needs to live and grow while also growing meat that has the texture and thickness we've become accustomed to?

'The challenge for the industry is that we really don't have a good proxy for what scaling looks like for these kinds of tissue structures. Flowing nutrient media through an actual fixed tissue [...] There's nothing at large scale that really looks like that,' says Specht. One possible solution would be to structure the maturing tissue so that it had plenty of gaps that nutrients could flow through and then, once the cells had developed into the right kinds of tissue, it could be compressed so it took on more of a meaty structure. Or meat could be grown in sheets, before being collected together for a final product. Another approach, being trialled by the Israel-based cultivated-meat firm Aleph Farms, is to grow blood vessels alongside other cell types, leading to a finished product with a texture that more closely resembles a cut of meat.[12] 'I think most companies are at the point of sophistication where they're recognising that they'll need multiple different cell types. Not just a single cell type on a scaffold, but really what I call a co-culture of multiple cell types,' says Specht.

But even if the cultivated-meat industry can crack these scientific quandaries, it is still facing an even more fundamental question. How does its environmental footprint stack up against our current methods of producing meat? Until the first pilot facilities start publishing details about their production emissions, we simply don't know how growing meat in factories compares to farms. One study from 2011 estimated that cultivated meat would produce 76–96 per cent fewer greenhouse-gas emissions and use 82–96 per cent less water, depending on the meat product.[13] A later study published in 2015 estimated that because of its higher energy demands, cultivated pork and poultry could end up producing higher emissions than some conventional farms, although its impact on the land would be lower.[14] But until we have large-scale cultivated-meat factories in use, any analysis has to rely on assumptions about the size of the factory, how much media it uses and where its energy supply comes from. Change any one of these variables and the footprint of cultivated meat may head up or down. Upside Foods' plant, which Valeti expects will open in 2021, should provide some answers where before only uncertainty existed. 'No one has built these facilities before, so when we build and operate it, we are going to learn something very new. And based on that, we'll have to continue to adapt the design [...] So we're optimistic but we're not out of the woods yet,' he says.

The plant-protein alternative

While Valeti finally gears up to put his production plans to the test with his Berkeley plant, 1,200 kilometres to the north-east another potential solution to the planet's protein crisis has been biding its time in one of the most inhospitable environments on Earth.

Yellowstone National Park in Wyoming sits atop one of the world's largest volcanic systems. Hidden tens of kilometres under the park's surface are two giant chambers of magma that force water back to the Earth's surface until it spews out into geysers or rainbow-coloured hot springs. The extreme environment of these pools, where acidity levels can match those of stomach acid, are enough to kill most organisms that are unlucky enough to drop into the waters, but some microscopic organisms have managed to use the deadly environment to their advantage. In 2009 Mark Kozubal, then a PhD student at nearby Montana State University, was searching in a Yellowstone geyser basin for algae that could be turned into biofuel. What he ended up finding was a fungus that is preternaturally gifted at turning plant matter into protein: precisely the kind of organism that could help solve the world's growing demand for meat.

Today, the fungus that Kozubal plucked out of that geyser basin is used to make Fy – a protein-rich substance that forms long, meaty filaments as it grows. The company that Kozubal co-founded to develop Fy, called Nature's Fynd, is now split between a research and development facility in Bozeman, Montana, and a 3,250-square-metre production facility in Chicago's stockyards, the heart of what used to be the city's meat-packing district. Now, on land that used to be filled with pig pens, Fy is being grown in chambers, each one the size of a walk-in wardrobe and stacked with trays where the fungus sits on top of a source of sugar and other nutrients. Kozubal estimates that each chamber can produce about 15 tonnes of Fy a year. 'Because it evolved under tremendous evolutionary pressure it's a master at doing more with less – that's what you've got to do when you evolve in the volcanic acid springs at Yellowstone,' says Thomas Jonas, Nature's Fynd's CEO and co-founder.

Of course Fy isn't the only alternative protein on the menu. In China, protein-rich meat substitutes have been eaten for millennia. Early versions of tofu, produced by coagulating soy milk, were being eaten in the third century AD, and by the tenth century it had gained a nickname that emphasised its meat-replacing credentials – *xiao zaiyang* – which means 'small mutton'. Meanwhile in the West various other start-ups are making their own bids to produce plant-based meat alternatives. In the past, plant-based protein has often meant dry bean-burgers and claggy patties made of mushed-up vegetables. These early plant-based burgers were so detached from their meat analogues that, unlike meat, they didn't require cooking so much as simply being heated up, explains Amy Rowat, a biophysicist at the University of California, Los Angeles, who teaches a lecture series about the science of food. But alongside companies like Nature's Fynd, a new cohort of plant-based start-ups is overturning this old veggie-burger cliché.

For nearly five years California-based start-up Impossible Foods worked to perfect a vegan alternative to the hamburger, one that packed the umami punch and metallic tang of the real thing. Despite being one of the best-funded food start-ups in recent history (including a snubbed acquisition attempt from Google), Impossible Foods had managed to keep its product development under wraps, testing prototype burgers from undercover food trucks.[15] In July 2016 it launched the Impossible Burger at the trendy Momufuku Nishi restaurant in Manhattan. Its arrival was greeted by dozens of articles marvelling at what until then seemed unthinkable: a veggie-burger that oozed like a medium-rare hunk of beef. 'With this new generation of plant-based burgers, you get these more sophisticated changes in colour and texture that happen upon cooking,' says Rowat.

At a glance, the ingredient list of the Impossible Burger is nothing unusual. It's mostly made of soy protein, water, coconut oil, sunflower oil, a few binding agents and flavourings, plus a sprinkling of vitamins and minerals usually found in meat. But what makes the Impossible Burger different from most of its predecessors is haem – an iron-containing molecule found in animal muscles that gives ground beef its colour and slightly metallic taste. In muscle, haem is found in a protein called myoglobin, but it's also found in the roots of soy plants, which carry a version of the molecule called leghaemoglobin. While extracting the leghaemoglobin directly from soy itself would use 0.4 hectares of land to produce just a kilogram of the molecule, Impossible's founder Patrick Brown took the gene that codes for the production of leghaemoglobin and inserted it into yeast, which can manufacture the molecule using far less land than either cattle or soy.[16] All this adds up to a burger that, according to Impossible Foods, produces 89 per cent fewer emissions while using 87 per cent less water and 96 per cent land than its cow-based equivalent.[17]

Of course creating a more environmentally friendly burger means nothing unless people are actually eating it. But there are signs that the new generation of plant-based meat – including the Beyond Burger, whose meaty texture comes from the way pea protein is heated and squeezed as the burger is made – is finding traction where decades of bean-burgers failed to thrill. Between 2017 and 2019 sales of plant-based meat in the US grew by 37.8 per cent to $939 million (£717 million). In the UK, 2019 saw the launch of plant-based meat options from KFC, Burger King, Subway and the bakery chain Greggs, whose vegan sausage roll contributed to a 13 per cent bump in the firm's stock price in the first quarter of the year.[18] When the Covid-19 pandemic hit the US, the loud, cramped environs of meat-packing plants became a focal point for outbreaks. In April 2020 alone, a dozen meat-packing plants in the US had to shut due to outbreaks among employees. Plant-based meat suppliers rushed to fill the gaps on meat aisles with their own alternatives, in the hope of enticing customers who wouldn't have looked twice at a veggie-burger until the choice became plant-based meat or no meat at all. This, perhaps, is the biggest shift with this new generation of plant-based burgers. Although many of its greatest advocates shun meat altogether (both Patrick Brown and Beyond Meat's CEO Ethan Brown follow vegan diets), these products aren't just meant for vegetarians – they're firmly aimed at the multi-trillion-dollar global meat industry. That is where the real impact lies.

Despite its new wunderkinds, we're still in the early days of plant-based meat. In the US, sales of plant-based meat account for just 1 per cent of all retail meat sales.[19] Compared to plant-based milk alternatives, which now account for 14 per cent of retail milk sales, meat alternatives have a long way to go. They are also facing resistance along the way. In 2018 the US state of Missouri made a tweak to its advertising laws that required plant-based meat brands to include a 'prominent statement' that the product was made from plants and not animals. In response, several plant-based meat advocacy groups teamed up with the brand Tofurky to launch a lawsuit challenging the law as unconstitutional. In Europe similar regulations prevent plant-based milks, cheeses and yoghurts being described using those words. The lab-grown meat industry has had related problems knowing what to call itself. In the past it flirted with calling its products clean, cell-based and cultured. For the moment, the in-vogue nomenclature is 'cultivated'. How much naming matters to consumers, however, is yet to be seen.

While cultivated-meat start-ups wonder what to call the meat of the future, the meat industry itself is coming round to the idea that the future of protein isn't just about animals. In 2019 the United States' biggest meat producer, Tyson Foods, launched a line of part-meat-part-plant products that includes burgers made of a blend of Angus beef and pea protein. Ultimately it's likely that each of these approaches – cultivated, plant-based and blended – will fill a separate niche in the vast meat industry. Liz Specht at the Good Food Institute thinks that while the first cultivated-meat products that make it to supermarket shelves will be ground beef and other processed meats, in the long run that approach will be better suited to steaks and other kinds of highly structured meats that can command a much higher price. 'Plant-based will be good enough for a lot of the minced-meat or processed-meat products that there might not be as much incentive to make through a slightly more sophisticated cultivated-meat platform,' she says. Getting to that point, however, will require a lot more fundamental research when it comes to figuring out how to structure cuts of meat, combine different cell types together and grow them in a bioreactor.

That may prove to be a challenge. Although the world of cultivated meat has moved on a lot since Mark Post received that cheque from Sergey Brin, almost all of that progress has been funded by private backers or organisations that rely on donations. Isha Datar, the executive director of New Harvest, a non-profit research organisation that has been instrumental in developing the early alternative protein industry, acknowledges that although the world of cultivated meat is starting to flesh out, it is nowhere near as developed as the agricultural or meat industries, which have benefited from decades of government support and publicly funded research. 'I think the fact that there is no pipeline for talent into cellular agriculture today is a big problem,' she says. 'You can't meet a high-school student and they say, "Okay, I'm going to get a Masters in cellular agriculture and then I'm going to work in industry." That is still a non-existent pathway.' Changing the way the world eats will require more than just a few dozen well-meaning start-ups. 'I think governments need to recognise that this is a new field of research that is neither food science in the traditional sense nor tissue engineering in the traditional sense,' Datar says. 'Only once we see that recognition and that government support do I think we can have a big pipeline towards industry support.'

In many parts of the world, however, governments aren't thinking about upending the way we produce protein. They are more preoccupied with saving the food we already have from disappearing altogether.

2

Improving crops

Hans Bhardwaj grew up hungry. Born in 1952 in a village in the foothills of the Himalayas in the Indian state of Himachal Pradesh, Bhardwaj spent his childhood in a country teetering on the edge of famine. In the summer of 1965 the monsoon failed, starting a two-year-long drought that caused crops to wilt and food prices to skyrocket. The outbreak of war with Pakistan in August of that year served to make matters even worse, and also prompted an America already antagonised by India's opposition to the US war in Vietnam to threaten to suspend vital wheat shipments. The situation became so desperate that, in a bid to stretch the country's meagre food resources even further, India's prime minister, Lal Bahadur Shastri, took to All India Radio to ask Indians to skip at least one meal a week.

Just three years later the picture would be dramatically reversed. In 1968 India recorded such large harvests that staff at the State Department in Washington DC were completely taken aback. 'Unprecedentedly large 1968 wheat crop moving rapidly to market is straining facilities,' came the cable from the US embassy in New Delhi. With railway freight cars overwhelmed, school buildings, sugar mills and theatres were commandeered by the government to store the excess grain. In 1964 the country had produced 79 million tonnes of food. By 1968 that figure had jumped by over one-fifth to 95 million tonnes, in a bumper year that saw the country produce one-third more wheat than it had ever grown before.[1]

Much of this wave of productivity was down to new high-yielding strains of rice and wheat developed by the International Rice Research Institute (IRRI) in Los Baños, in the Philippines, and the International Maize and Wheat Improvement Center (CIMMYT) in Mexico. Aided by the adoption of new machines, chemical fertilisers, pesticides and irrigation systems, the high-yielding varieties were growing like nothing farmers had seen before. 'It made a huge difference, it saved so many lives and avoided famine,' says Bhardwaj, who now heads the rice breeding platform at IRRI. One rice variety, officially called IR8, was often given the nickname 'miracle rice', thanks to its bountifulness. Developed by breeding together a sturdy, short Taiwanese rice with a tall, high-yielding rice from Indonesia, IR8 could produce up to ten tonnes of crop per hectare of farmland – almost double that of the rice previously grown in India.[2] One farmer in south-east India was so impressed by his increased yields that he named his son Irettu – Tamil for IR8.

What the researchers at IRRI and CIMMYT had harnessed was the power of selective breeding – the science of choosing individual plants with desirable traits, such as resistance to disease or short stalks to stop the plant toppling over in the wind, and breeding them together to produce offspring that combine both of the useful attributes of its parents. Humans have been selectively breeding plants for at least 10,000 years. Corn, for example, began as a weedy wild grass with a handful of tough kernels, before being bred over hundreds of years to become the plant we recognise today. But the process of improvement became turbocharged after the Second World War when scientists led by the American agronomist Norman Borlaug and funded by the Rockefeller Foundation began to breed new high-yielding and disease-resistant crop varieties that grew bountifully when paired with modern agricultural technology such as chemical fertilisers. The result was what became known as the Green Revolution: a leap forward in crop productivity worldwide. Between 1961 and 2000 in Mexico – one of the earliest countries to benefit from the Green Revolution – cereal production more than tripled, while the land used for production of that crop went up by just one-third.[3] In 1970 Borlaug won the Nobel Peace Prize for his efforts. As the scientist sat in the auditorium at the University of Oslo in Norway waiting to receive his award, the chair of the Nobel Committee, Aase Lionæs, described him as the person who, 'more than any other single person of this age, has helped to provide bread for a hungry world'.

Fifty years later, the gains of the Green Revolution are starting to stall. Even by the 1990s the average annual growth in rice yield in Asia had fallen to just 1.1 per cent, down from 2.7 per cent in the 1960s. Today in China and Indonesia, two of the world's three biggest rice-producing countries, rice yields are flat or declining across nearly four-fifths of farmland.[4] The picture is similar for other major crops, including wheat and corn.

It's not just that the Green Revolution is losing its edge. A deadly combination of increased temperatures, new pests and diseases and more erratic weather is putting the productivity of farmland under extreme pressure. In southern Bangladesh nearly 40 per cent of productive land is threatened by rising sea levels, which leak salt water into fields, killing off rice and other crops.[5] There, many farmers face a tough decision: abandon their fields altogether or else convert them into shrimp farms and try their luck at an industry more resistant to rising sea levels.

A genetic way forward?

Hans Bhardwaj at IRRI is hoping that the answer to the problems facing the world's rice fields today lies in the sheer variety of rice there is out there. In IRRI's Los Baños headquarters, a room holds the International Rice Genebank – a store of more than 132,000 rice varieties, which includes domesticated rice from all over the world and more than 4,000 wild-rice varieties. Seeds in the long-term collection are stored at minus 20 degrees Celsius to preserve them for later use. To protect the genebank in case disaster strikes, backup collections are stored in Fort Collins, Colorado, and at the Svalbard Global Seed Vault in the remote Norwegian Arctic archipelago. 'Our assumption is that if we have this collection of rice from all over the world they would have almost all the variability that we would be interested in today or tomorrow,' says Bhardwaj. 'Any variation which you are looking for, it already exists somewhere in nature.'

Within IRRI's collection there are rice varieties that have adapted to use less water as they grow – useful in a world where rainfall is less reliable. Others are naturally resistant to certain pests and diseases, and some can withstand salt levels that would cause most varieties to wilt. Much remains to be done, and the work is slow and painstaking, but IRRI is methodically sequencing the genome of each and every variety. So far the organisation has sequenced 3,000 varieties and found 1,000 different genetic markers of certain plant qualities that warrant further investigation. 'We are trying to analyse and understand at a genetic level each and every one of those [varieties], but we have a long way to go to complete that,' says Bhardwaj.

Once researchers identify beneficial traits, they can breed lines together to create new varieties. It's a process that used to take Bhardwaj at least a decade, but new intensive growing techniques that speed up the time it takes to grow new varieties help cut down the risk that researchers will squander precious time focusing on a variety that ends up not being used. By growing plants in greenhouses with tightly controlled temperatures and lights, researchers at IRRI have doubled the number of rice generations that can be grown within a single year. 'With new technologies and advances, we are now shooting for anything between four to six years [per variety],' he says.

These techniques are already paying off. In India and Bangladesh, flooding destroys four million tonnes of rice each year – enough to feed 30 million people.[6] But in 2006 scientists isolated a gene from an unusual ancient rice variety that enabled the plants to tolerate being underwater for more than two weeks. A new variety incorporating this gene was developed by Pamela Ronald at the University of California, Davis, in collaboration with IRRI, and can survive being submerged in floodwater for ten days, helping farmers weather severe floods without writing off their entire crops. This so-called 'Scuba rice' is already being grown by millions of farmers in Asia – just one more checkpoint in the endless race between climate change and crop science.

While rice is facing a number of threats – flooding, salt water and droughts – the sheer number of varieties out there means that scientists like Ronald and Bhardwaj have a rich trove of genetic diversity to dig through to breed the ideal rice for every situation. If a new variety isn't quite hitting the spot, they can always cross it with an existing plant, or try a variety that was originally bred for use elsewhere in the world.

Not every plant has such a rich pool of genetic diversity to fall back on. Saving the Cavendish banana, for example, will mean reaching for an even more powerful set of plant-tweaking tools. These, however, raise scientific and ethical questions about future food production that we have yet to answer.

If you're reading this book in Europe or the US, there's a good chance that every single banana you've ever eaten is a descendant of the same handful of plants grown in the mid-1830s in an English greenhouse belonging to the sixth Duke of Devonshire. There are more than 1,000 banana varieties in existence – the Brazilian apple banana, for example, is small and tart with firm flesh, while the stubby Pisang Awak, a staple in Malaysia, is much sweeter and can be used for brewing beer. But none of these bananas can come close to matching the ubiquity of the Cavendish. From its start as a horticultural curiosity in a single English greenhouse, the Cavendish banana now makes up 99 per cent of the entire global export market for the fruit. In the UK more than five billion bananas are bought every single year; almost every single one of them is a Cavendish.[7]

The reason the Cavendish has been so successful is partly down to its genetics. Since the plant has three copies of each chromosome, it is sterile and can only reproduce by creating genetically identical copies of itself. For farmers, this is exceptionally handy. It means they know exactly how each plant will respond to pesticides, how quickly its fruit will ripen and how they will handle the bumpy journey thousands of kilometres across the ocean from Latin America. But this is also the Cavendish's fatal flaw. Since every plant is genetically identical, each one is also vulnerable to the exact same diseases. And in the case of the Cavendish, it is facing a particularly nasty foe.

In 1989 a plant pathologist at the University of Florida named Randy Ploetz received the first sample of a fungus that would become the biggest threat currently facing the world's bananas. Tropical Race 4 (TR4) is a strain of the fungus *Fusarium oxysporum cubense* that lives in soil and hitch-hikes its way between banana plantations on muddy boots, tyres and planting equipment. Once it has found its way into a field, TR4 enters the roots of banana plants and clogs up their vascular systems, starving them of water and nutrients until the plants stop producing fruit and eventually die. Fields infected with TR4 are usually abandoned as the fungus can live in soil for up to 30 years, impervious to pesticides. Since Ploetz analysed that first sample of infected soil, TR4 has been making its way around the globe at an alarming pace. Already widespread in South East Asia, the fungus has also been found in Lebanon, Israel, India, Jordan, Oman, Pakistan and Australia. In August 2019 it was discovered in four banana plantations in Colombia – the third-biggest banana exporter in the world and a linchpin of the global banana industry. When the Colombian government announced that the fungus had been found on its soil, it declared a national state of emergency.

The banana industry has been here before. In the 1950s, before the Cavendish came to dominate the export market, the Gros Michel was the banana of choice for Europeans and Americans – a creamier, sweeter banana that by most accounts was tastier than the fruit that succeeded it. But the Gros Michel was also susceptible to a different strain of the *Fusarium* fungus, Tropical Race 1 (TR1). After being discovered in Latin America in 1890, TR1 ripped through banana plantations until the major producers had no other choice than to switch to their backup banana, the less delicious but, crucially, TR1-resistant Cavendish. In 1960 the world's largest banana exporter, United Fruit Company (now called Chiquita), began switching to the Cavendish, following the lead of its smaller rival, Standard Fruit Company (now called Dole), which switched in 1947. By the mid-1960s Gros Michel – or 'Big Mike', as it was also called – was nowhere to be seen on supermarket shelves in the West.

Now scientists and start-ups are racing to save the Cavendish from going the same way as the Gros Michel. In 2004 James Dale, a professor at Queensland University of Technology in Australia, isolated a gene from a wild cousin of the Cavendish called *Musa acuminata malaccensis*. Although the banana was unlikely to find itself as a cereal topper – each fruit is filled with upwards of 60 hard seeds – it does have one major advantage over the Cavendish: a gene that makes it naturally resistant to TR4. Dale used bacteria to shuttle this gene from *Musa acuminata malaccensis* into the Cavendish plant and planted a field of test crops in 2012. Three years later the results were in. By the end of the trial, between 67 and 100 per cent of the plants without the resistance gene (called RGA2) had been killed or infected with TR4. Of the five test crops with the added gene, four had much lower rates of infection – below 30 per cent – and one had no signs of the disease at all.[8] Dale is currently running another field study on the bananas, which is already showing extremely promising results. Once that trial ends in 2021, he plans to apply to regulators for approval to market the banana in Australia.

However, despite managing to make a banana that seems to be resistant to TR4, Dale's fruits are unlikely to make it out of Australia. Because they contain genetic material from two different organisms (in this case, two types of banana), they are classified by most regulators as genetically modified (GM) organisms, which will make it extremely difficult to market them to consumers in Europe and elsewhere. Dozens of countries, including China, Russia, Japan, Australia, Brazil and the European Union (EU), legally require GM food to be labelled. Despite being relatively common in the US, GM fruits and vegetables are currently not sold in the EU. Once vaunted by plant scientists as a faster and more precise alternative to selective breeding, the reputation of GM crops has been battered by suspicions about their health and environmental impacts, and the motivations of companies that make the varieties. In June 1998 an episode of the British current-affairs TV programme *World in Action* featured an interview with a Hungarian biochemist who claimed to have found that rats eating GM potatoes had stunted growth and suppressed immune systems. These findings were later discredited and scientists have been unable to find any long-term health impacts linked to consumption of genetically modified food – a stance endorsed by the World Health Organization and the American Medical Association – but for large swathes of the world decades of negative press have turned popular opinion resolutely against GM food.

A start-up in Norwich in the UK is attempting to sidestep the furore over GM food by using a new gene-editing technique to fix the Cavendish's fatal flaw. Tropic Biosciences is growing Cavendish plants that have been edited using CRISPR-Cas9 (CRISPR for short) – a DNA-editing molecule that can tweak the genetic code of a plant or animal without the need to insert genetic information from another organism. 'Globally there are more and more regulators that are recognising the absolute need to solve some of these problems, and that gene editing is probably the best and quickest way to do it,' says Gilad Gershon, Tropic's CEO.

Gershon is taking a two-pronged approach to defeating TR4. First, he's trying to target genes in the Cavendish plant that make it susceptible to the fungus and reduce their activity, using CRISPR. Second, he's trying to get the plants to fight back against the fungus as well. All plants produce strands of a molecule called ribonucleic acid (RNA) that controls how certain genes are expressed – either telling the cell to ramp up the action of that gene or silencing it entirely. But some of this RNA can cross from the plant and into microorganisms that are attacking the plant, silencing genes in the invaders too.[9] The scientists at Tropic Biosciences are hoping that, by editing the Cavendish plant, they will be able to render TR4 completely harmless.

After fixing the problem of TR4-susceptibility once with his GM bananas, James Dale is now also using

CRISPR to create a Cavendish that is TR4-resistant and sidesteps GM regulations, but with a slightly different approach to Gershon. His plan is to try and turn on a dormant gene in Cavendish bananas that confers resistance to TR4 – the same gene he took from *Musa acuminata malaccensis* for his genetically modified variety. In the US such an approach is regarded by the Department of Agriculture as very different from GM food. CRISPR has already been used to create mushrooms that are resistant to browning and don't fall under the Department's rules for GM foods.

The EU has a very different view on CRISPR. On 25 July 2018 Europe's highest court dealt a blow to the future of CRISPR-edited bananas. After being asked in 2016 by the French government to clarify how a 15-year-old directive on genetically modified crops applied to ones created using modern gene-editing techniques, the European Court of Justice ruled that CRISPR-edited crops would not be exempt from existing regulations limiting the cultivation and sale of GM organisms. In the eyes of the EU, there was not much difference between Dale's transgenic bananas and a CRISPR-edited banana after all.

This decision might not matter an awful lot to someone in the EU – until it means that their beloved bananas disappear from shelves – but if it has the effect of stalling research into CRISPR-edited crops, then it could shut off vital future sources of food for people in less developed parts of the world. In some areas of Uganda bananas provide up to 25 per cent of people's daily calories. 'I think this doesn't take into account the massive need to improve productivity that we face,' says Gershon. Of the two billion people that the UN expects will be added to the planet's population by 2050, half of them will be born in Africa. If we don't use the tools available to us, Gershon comments, then it is the developing world that will bear the brunt of the fallout.

In a purpose-built facility in Norwich the scientists at Tropic Biosciences are already testing their plants for TR4 resistance. Other researchers are also trying to use CRISPR to give the Cavendish a fighting chance. At the International

Institute of Tropical Agriculture in Nairobi, Kenya, a molecular biologist named Leena Tripathi is using the gene-editing technique to suppress genes in the Cavendish that seem to make it vulnerable to TR4.[10] The technology is also being used to make tomatoes that are easier to harvest, and orange trees that are resistant to disease.

Despite these tantalising results, the future path of CRISPR-edited food, for now, is far from straightforward. But in large swathes of the world farmers can't afford to wait for high-yielding and gene-edited crops to run the gamut of scientific trials and regulatory approval, they're still waiting for the benefits of the Green Revolution to come their way.

Rich and poor farmers: levelling the field

For the past half-century farmers from all over the US have congregated each spring to witness the crowning of the winner of a prestigious competition: the National Corn Yield Contest. In 2019, 7,454 corn farmers paid their entry dues, brushed up on the 17-page-long list of rules and requirements and prepared to leverage every high-yielding variety, herbicide, insecticide, fungicide, fertiliser and precision irrigation tool they had, in order to make their corn field the most productive in the US. The National Corn Yield Contest is in some ways the exaggerated endpoint of the Green Revolution – a place where the only aim is to squeeze as much food out of the land as possible.

In 2019 the champion of the National Corn Yield Contest was David Hula, who managed to push his farm in Charles City, Virginia, to produce 38.7 tonnes per hectare – his fourth world record for corn harvests.[11] His son, Craig, took third place in the competition with 34.3 tonnes per hectare. For Hula, whose yield was more than three-and-a-half times the average in the US that year, his results indicated that, with the right management tools and perfect timing, there is still plenty of untapped potential in the crops we have today. 'If that [yield] limit is, say, 800 or 900 bushels per acre [50 or 55 tonnes per hectare], and the country-wide average is only 170 bushels per acre [10.7 tonnes per hectare], we have a long way to go,' he told *Progressive Farmer* magazine after his victory.

If the National Corn Yield Contest is a techno-optimist vision of where the world could be headed, to get a sense of what is really holding back the productivity of the world's fields you need to travel an ocean away to the resource-starved corn fields of sub-Saharan Africa. Corn is one of the African continent's most important crops. In low-income households across Africa, it accounts for between 30 and 50 per cent of total household expenditure, and for those living in sub-Saharan Africa the crop makes up more than 30 per cent of total daily calories. Despite the continent's reliance on corn, even a bad year on David Hula's farm would be the stuff of fantasy for most African farmers. In Nigeria, Africa's second-biggest grower of corn, average yields are just 1.6 tonnes per hectare, less than one-sixth of the average American yield. While the

Green Revolution saw yields shoot upwards in the rest of the world, particularly in Latin America and Asia, sub-Saharan Africa missed out almost entirely on these benefits. A 2008 report from the World Bank showed that the region lagged significantly behind every other region when it came to access to irrigation, improved varieties of cereals and fertilisers.[12]

The problem for the region isn't that the technology to get more out of the soil doesn't exist, it's that farmers can't get their hands on it, says Abdulai Jalloh, director of research and innovation at the West and Central African Council for Agricultural Research and Development in Dakar, Senegal. 'That's the issue. Because [farmers] don't have resources, they cannot buy inputs, so they can't capitalise on the innovations that are available to them,' he says. 'Governments need to build infrastructure that the private sector cannot [...] roads, bridges, water, electricity, schools, hospitals that enable other players to come in and provide services.' Climate change is also adding pressure to an already difficult situation.

According to the Intergovernmental Panel on Climate Change, a decline in rainfall and increase in droughts in West Africa could shorten growing seasons by an average of 20 per cent by 2050, causing a 40 per cent decline in cereal yields across the region.[13]

Despite the challenges facing the continent today, the potential of sub-Saharan Africa is huge. A report from the consulting group McKinsey & Company estimated that if crop production was intensified in sub-Saharan Africa, total cereal production could increase to two or three times its current levels. 'Because of the land and the agroecology, the region can definitely be food-secure. No doubt about that. You don't even need to expand [land use],' says Jalloh. Making the region food-secure will mean finding a way to supply smallholder farms with the resources they need to increase production. Smallholder farms of a few hectares or less make up 80 per cent of farms in sub-Saharan Africa and, in some countries, provide as much as 90 per cent of food production. The Kenya-based non-profit One Acre Fund has been helping to increase the productivity of smallholder farms in East Africa for 14 years. The company provides loan-backed resources and training to more than a million farmers to help them improve the productivity of their land. In 2019 the organisation helped farmers in Rwanda increase their income by 81 per cent – a difference of $34 (£26) a year.

By boosting the productivity of smallholder farms, the One Acre Fund is trying to fix one of the biggest problems facing today's food system: food itself is not evenly distributed across the globe. 'One of the problems that people don't talk enough about is that the problem of food insecurity is a problem of poverty – it's not a problem of insufficient food at a global level,' says Hannah Wittman, professor of land and food systems at the University of British Columbia in Canada. Money in the food world, she says, mostly flows towards market opportunities and not towards attempts to address hunger. Investment in plant-based burgers and genetically modified soybeans might be useful, but ultimately they go towards feeding the parts of the world that already have enough to eat, and not towards the 746 million people who went hungry in 2020. The disruption to food-supply chains and economic upheaval caused by the Covid-19 pandemic are set to make things even worse, adding between 83 and 132 million more undernourished people to that total. In Africa, while investment has flowed towards wheat, soybean and other commodity crops, indigenous foods are often underfunded, even though crops such as cowpea, with its tolerance for sandy soil and low rainfall, could be particularly useful in a world made hotter and drier by climate change.[14]

Building more resilient food networks in the developing world will mean helping smallholders become more productive, investing in sustainable agriculture and supporting farm workers, particularly women, who make up almost half of the agricultural labour force in sub-Saharan Africa. Wittman points to the Fome Zero (Zero Hunger) programme put in place by the then-president of Brazil Luiz Inácio Lula da Silva in 2003 as one example of a government helping small farmers effectively. The programme included a scheme where the Brazilian government bought food directly from family farmers to serve in public facilities, and introduced a law requiring 30 per cent of food for school meals to come from family farms. The government also backed schemes to capture more rainwater and provide food and equipment to restaurants, community kitchens and food banks. In 2014 the World Food Programme removed Brazil from its 'hunger map' of countries with large proportions of undernourished citizens. 'They made all of these investments, and they vastly improved their food security, vastly improved income inequality and environmental outcomes on many farms,' says Wittman.

The Fome Zero campaign powerfully demonstrates that improving food networks is a potent weapon in the battle to feed the planet. But even when combined with breeding methods and gene-editing techniques it's not enough, given the environmental challenges facing the world. While crop scientists are racing to be able to feed two billion extra people by 2050, unless we can get on top of farming's environmental footprint, we risk bringing them into a world that is less stable and productive than what went before. Faced with this dilemma, a new generation of farmers and thinkers is attempting to untangle the Gordian knot that ties together climate change and food, and steer us away from a food system that churns through freshwater and fossil-fuel reserves while also chucking fertiliser and pesticides into the environment. For them, the future of food isn't simply a matter of producing more – it's about using *less*.

3

Reducing farming's footprint

Weeds are nature's ultimate survivors. The seeds of the common lambsquarters weed, for example, can survive for so long in the ground that viable seeds have been plucked from medieval ruins. Parasitic dodder weeds insert themselves into the stems of other plants, building bridges between their unwilling hosts and transmitting messages between them that warn when one is being attacked by insects. Others opt for safety in numbers: a single ragweed plant can release up to one billion pollen grains, each one floating as far as 650 kilometres in search of a flower to pollinate, causing major problems for hayfever sufferers.

Out of all the weeds, however, nothing rankles with farmers like pigweed. Thick-stemmed and bushy, pigweed is a master at digging in where it is least welcome and at filching nutrients and water from its neighbours. A single plant can produce between 200,000 and 600,000 seeds that take root within a day or two of hitting the soil and then grow at a prodigious speed, eventually reaching heights of more than three metres. In 2014 Clint Brauer was helping out on his father's soybean farm in Kansas during what was set to be a bumper year for the crop. 'The soybean was chest-high. They were huge and it was going to be an amazing yield,' he says. The only problem was that the field was infested with pigweed. Things soon became so bad that Clint's father had to hire a crew of farmhands to hack, slash and pull the plants from the field. They quit within 15 minutes. 'The world's strongest man is not going to pull a six-foot-tall pigweed out of the ground,' says Brauer. 'It was a disaster.'

Most farmers, however, don't opt for brute force as their first weed-management tool. Instead, they turn to herbicides. Humans have been waging chemical warfare on weeds for millennia, but the herbicide industry didn't get started in earnest until the Second World War, when American researchers investigating potential biological weapons realised that the chemicals they were testing could also be used to selectively kill weeds. By 1962 farmers were using the new herbicides to treat more than 28 million hectares of farmland. Twelve years later the agricultural firm Monsanto released a herbicide based on a chemical called glyphosate, which worked by blocking the production of proteins that plants use to grow and repair themselves. Marketed under the name Roundup, the weedkiller was almost too successful: it killed pretty much every plant it came into contact with, good or bad. Monsanto's really genius move came a couple of decades later when, in the mid-1990s, the firm managed to create genetically modified crops that were resistant to glyphosate. Marketed as Roundup Ready, these crops enabled farmers to spray the herbicide indiscriminately without the risk of harming their modified soy, corn or cotton. Within a decade, 90 per cent of all US soybean was genetically modified to be glyphosate-resistant and the total amount of the herbicide being used by farmers had increased by more than six times. Despite being linked to an increased risk of some cancers, glyphosate is still the world's most-used herbicide.[1]

Unfortunately for farmers, weeds have started fighting back. In 2005 researchers at the University of Georgia found glyphosate-resistant pigweed growing in a cotton farm two hours south of Atlanta. Most plants have two copies of the gene that codes for the protein blocked by glyphosate, but glyphosate-resistant pigweed has between five and 160 copies, allowing it to withstand several times the amount of herbicide that would wipe out any non-resistant plant. In March 2019 farmers received even more bad news. Pigweed resistant to two other widely used herbicides, dicamba and 2,4-D, had been found in a field in north-east Kansas. Today herbicide-resistant pigweed is growing across an estimated 18 million hectares of farms in 39 US states.[2] Three plant biologists writing in the academic journal *Science* in 2018 warned that humans may lose the fight against resistant weeds: 'There is [...] a considerable chance that the evolution of pest resistance will outpace human innovation.'[3]

The end of herbicides?

Faced with the onslaught of herbicide-resistant weeds, Clint Brauer thinks he may have come up with a solution: weed-chopping robots. At his farm in Cheney, Kansas, Brauer has built a fleet of ten machines that trundle autonomously through rows of soybean plants, mowing down any weeds they come across. The goal is eventually to convince farmers to trade in their herbicide-spraying rigs for a subscription to a fleet of automatons that can wipe out weeds without the need for any chemicals.

Despite being the son and grandson of farmers, Brauer had no intention of getting into the family trade. Instead, after studying at Kansas State University, he headed to Los Angeles in the middle of the dot-com bubble, working first for a web app-design company and later in the music industry. But after 13 years in Los Angeles, Brauer decided to return to Kansas and set up shop as an organic farmer, growing pesticide-free vegetables in greenhouses. 'I decided that whatever I do, I want to do something that no one can argue isn't good. And I also want to do something that's real and lasts,' he says. At the same time he was trying to convert his fields so that they no longer relied on tilling – churning over the top few centimetres of soil to bury weeds and prepare the farm for planting. The alternative, called no-till farming, is favoured by a growing number of farmers because it improves soil health and can cut down on the amount of carbon released from the ground.[4] But no-till farming has one big drawback. Weeds grow easily in the undisturbed soil, leaving farmers with little choice but to reach for the herbicides.

For Brauer, this was a compromise he didn't want to be forced into. So in 2015 he attached a rotary mower to the back of a tractor and started attacking every weed in sight. 'I could see that the more mature they were, when you were cutting them off, they really didn't come back very fast. And when they did, it was slower and slower. And by the third time you cut them, they are pretty much done,' he says. Two years later he pitched the idea of robotic weed mowers to Steven Getner, an old friend who had founded a machine-vision company called RoboRealm. Not long afterwards Getner and Brauer had their first prototype robot. 'We had [the robot] shipped to the farm and started running it. And of course it didn't work worth a damn [...] one started smoking within ten minutes in the field,' Brauer says.

Seventeen prototypes later, Greenfield Robotics, the company Brauer founded to bring his project to life, finally has a fleet of robots ready to be tested by farmers. Weighing roughly 60 kilograms, each device looks like a miniature dog kennel on wheels, with a tall pole sticking out of the back, housing communications equipment to stop the robot running off the edge of the field. As they run autonomously through rows of crops, the robots use machine vision to steer while the blades below spin constantly within a few centimetres of the crops – close enough to take out the majority of the most troublesome weeds. Brauer hopes that a pod of ten robots will be able to knock out about 40 hectares' worth of weeds in a single day. The robots still have the cobbled-together look of an after-hours science project, but Brauer doesn't need them to win a beauty contest as long as they work. If he's going to convince farmers to trade in their herbicide, Brauer will need to prove that the robots can perform the same job, just as reliably and without any extra cost. The Kansan is optimistic that once farmers start using his robots, they'll see the benefits and leave their herbicide-spraying equipment behind. After all, he says, no farmer really enjoys using herbicides. 'They want to keep their family going in the business. They're not attached to spray rigs.'

In England another start-up is taking Brauer's vision of robotic farming even further. Sam Watson-Jones is the co-founder of Small Robot Company, a Wiltshire-based start-up with its own fleet of autonomous farmhands. For him, the real potential of robots doesn't lie in their weed-whacking ability, but in their data-gathering skills. 'It's actually being able to completely digitise the field – turn it into a series of ones and zeros where you know the exact location and the exact status of every plant in that field, turning every plant into its own individual data point,' he says. Watson-Jones calls this approach 'per-plant farming', tracking exactly how each plant is doing so that it can receive precisely the inputs it needs to grow. Wheat plant looking a little scrawny? Deploy a robot to give it a shot of fertiliser. Weeds becoming a problem in an overlooked corner? No need to spray herbicide everywhere, just send a machine to deliver a jolt of electricity and zap it out of existence.

Small Robot Company's approach hinges on a simple premise: all plants do not grow equally. Yet large industrialised farms are built to deliver the same resources to every plant at the same time, usually by a farmer driving a tractor with a herbicide-spraying rig or manure spreader attached. 'The principal engineering consideration is how quickly can this machine cover the ground,' says

Watson-Jones. But take the human out of the loop and the most important part of the task is no longer time; it's accuracy. With the right data, and robots sophisticated enough to act on it, our entire approach to farming could go from one that encourages the overuse of fertilisers and herbicides to one where farmers only use exactly what is required. 'You're using less fertiliser because you're getting better data, so you're not just chucking it everywhere. You're understanding where exactly it needs to be applied,' says Watson-Jones. The hope is that this won't just save farmers money, but will stop excess chemicals spreading into the environment. More than one-third of all nitrogen fertilisers applied to croplands end up leaching into the oceans, where they lead to vast algal blooms that suck oxygen out of coastal waters, killing fish, turtles and other animals. In the Gulf of Mexico, fertiliser run-off from the Mississippi River contributes to vast ocean dead zones, nearly devoid of marine life, that can stretch for more than 20,000 square kilometres.[5]

If farmers are to cut down on fertiliser and other inputs, they'll need to be more precise with the resources they are putting on the soil, and that means having access to data that tells them what their farm requires. There are already sensors that can tell farmers all kinds of things about their fields: how tightly compacted the soil is; which bits are lacking in nutrients; and how wet other bits are getting. But at the moment most of these sensors are either hand-held or designed to remain permanently in one place. Watson-Jones is experimenting with attaching sensors to robots that can take a soil sample, tag the exact location and go back a week later to see how things have changed. In the future, the robots could even be trained to recognise visual indicators of nutrient or disease stress in the plant, adding another vital piece of data into the decision-making puzzle.

For now, however, Small Robot Company is starting with weeds. In late 2020 the company deployed a robot – a quad-bike-sized machine with a large overhanging boom – in the fields of paying customers for the first time. The device, which Watson-Jones calls Tom, travels at a little under 5.6 kilometres an hour using machine vision to identify weeds and create a map that farmers can use to help pinpoint herbicide applications. In 2021, Small Robot Company paired Tom with another robot called Dick that kills weeds by zapping them with electricity, boiling the plant from the inside out. Although their robots look very different, Watson-Jones and Brauer both share a philosophy: that the only way to reduce farming's environmental impact is to find a way to unhook the system from its resource-heavy roots.

Managing water

Water appears to be everywhere, but in many parts of the world this precious resource is in desperately short supply. There are two main reasons for this. First, much of it is in forms that we can't use. It's locked up in ice caps and glaciers, in briny seawater or inaccessible groundwater reserves. The rest – the world's lakes, reservoirs and river systems – make up just 0.26 per cent of all of the world's freshwater resources.[6] Second, while that tiny fraction of a fraction is actually still enough to meet all the world's water needs if it's in the right places, it is not. Some parts of the world – Brazil, for example, which has more than 12 per cent of the planet's freshwater and just 2.7 per cent of its population – have more than they need. Other parts of the world, such as the Middle East, India and North Africa, suffer from extreme water scarcity. Saudi Arabia is rapidly depleting the groundwater aquifers that make up almost all of its water reserves. According to some estimates, the country may have less than 20 years before it runs out of natural freshwater sources altogether.[7]

Israel is the big success story in the water-starved Middle East. Providing enough water for Israel's 9.3 million citizens has required a monumental combination of huge infrastructure projects, new technology and persuasion. In 1964 the country completed a gigantic network of pipes, canals and pumping stations to heave water from the Sea of Galilee at 210 metres below sea level to the Negev desert in the south of the country. When rerouting the country's largest freshwater lake proved insufficient, Israel built a network of desalination plants that filter the salt water from the Mediterranean and pipe it to cities. These plants now provide 55 per cent of the nation's domestic drinking water. Citizens, meanwhile, have been encouraged to match these efforts by installing low-volume shower heads and dual-flush toilets that reduce water usage. Yet despite all this, the squeeze on Israel's water supplies is only going to get worse. Decreasing rainfall and longer dry spells could see the country's available water drop by a quarter by the end of the century. For Israel's neighbours in the Middle East, the situation is even more dire. According to the World Bank, climate-related water scarcity will cost countries in the Middle East and North Africa an estimated 6–14 per cent of their GDP by 2050.[8]

Unfortunately for countries lacking in water, pressure on the world's freshwater supplies is only going to go up. The main culprit? Agriculture. Globally, about 70 per cent of all freshwater goes towards our food, and by 2050 – with two billion or so more people on the planet –

demand for water will be 20–30 per cent greater than it was in 2019.[9] So how can the world increase its food supply without overstretching its precious water resources? One answer might be to bring farms indoors, where their water footprint can be drastically reduced.

Thirty-three metres below the busy streets of Clapham, south London, there is a tunnel bathed in artificial light and filled with ceiling-high stacks of tiny plants. This is Growing Underground, a farm housed in 6,000 metres of underground tunnels originally built to shelter Londoners from falling bombs during the Second World War. Today a small section of these tunnels is being used for an experiment in futuristic farming: growing plants in extremely controlled environments that use just a fraction of the water needed in traditional farming.

Richard Ballard co-founded Growing Underground in 2012, raising more than £800,000 through the crowd-funding platform Crowdcube to fill the subterranean farm with growing shelves and low-energy LED lights, which stand in for the sunlight that plants need to grow.

By locating the farm deep underground, Ballard has created a farm where every single factor that influences plant growth can be tracked and tweaked, if necessary: humidity, air flow, temperature and carbon-dioxide levels. As with Small Robot Company's mission to digitise farmers' fields, Ballard is attempting to use data to corral the unruly mess of agriculture into something that can be neatly pinpointed, tracked and responded to over time.

Insulating his farm from the whims of weather gives Ballard another advantage: he can predict almost exactly how much crop he'll harvest and when it will be ready. Growing Underground specialises in microgreens, very young plants that are harvested before their leaves have fully developed. The tiny watercress, mustard leaves, broccoli and sunflower shoots grown in Clapham are packaged into salad kits and sold in shops around the UK, or bought by high-end restaurants to add the finishing touches to haute-cuisine dishes. Starting as a seed, each plant spends between two and nine days germinating in a dark, humid section of the tunnel, before being moved to the main growing room where it grows on a substrate made from carpet offcuts. After spending up to 20 days growing under LED lights, the plants are ready to be harvested, packaged and sent to distribution centres the same day. 'Generally it's consistent. That enables us to be very accurate with supply and demand for customers. As we take new customers on, we know exactly how much we predict to bring out on a daily basis,' says Ballard.

The process also uses very little water. Ballard's farm uses a technique called hydroponics, whereby plants are grown in nutrient-rich water that is constantly cycled around the farm to ensure that every drop is maximally used. The trays of microgreens are filled with water, which gradually ebbs away during the day back to tanks on a lower level of the tunnel. This water is then filtered, treated with more nutrients and cycled back up to the plants upstairs, which means that the entire system uses 70 per cent less water than open-field agriculture, according to Growing Underground's own estimates. Bringing farms indoors not only reduces their water footprint, but also means they can be much closer to the distribution centres they eventually end up at. Ballard imagines a future where large food distribution centres will have vertical farms built next to them, selling ultra-fresh vegetables harvested moments before departure. In some places that vision is already coming true. The German vertical-farming firm Infarm already has more than 600 of its own growing units in stores and distribution centres across Europe, the US and Canada.

There is just one drawback: substituting the sun's rays with LED lights is extremely energy-intensive. According to analysis by Neil Mattson, a horticulturist at Cornell University in the US, plants grown on a vertical farm in New York City had more than double the energy cost and carbon footprint of plants grown on an outdoor farm in California and trucked 4,700 kilometres. Ballard is well aware of this major downside: it's the main reason his farm focuses on microgreens, which grow quickly and command a higher price per kilo, rather than on cheaper vegetables such as lettuce.

Despite these hurdles, there are places where hyper-local farming could make a lot of sense, particularly if the farms are hooked up to a source of renewable energy. In Newark, New Jersey, the headquarters of the indoor farming firm AeroFarms is home to a 6,500-square-metre farm capable of producing more than 900,000 kilograms of leafy greens annually. In July 2020 the company announced a deal to build ten vertical farms throughout care homes, schools, public housing and government buildings across Jersey City, in a scheme designed to provide local communities with free, locally grown greens. In the United Arab Emirates, one of the world's most water-stressed countries, AeroFarms has agreed to build an 8,300-square-metre indoor farm – the largest of its kind anywhere in the world.

It's important, however, not to overplay the potential of vertical farms. Most farmland is devoted to growing wheat, soy, corn and other commodity crops that simply cannot be produced at scale under LED lights in indoor farms. But when it comes to fruit and vegetables, hydroponics could help bring food production back into the urban areas where most of the world's population live, while cutting that food's water footprint.

Helping insects

While managing weeds and water remain two of the biggest challenges facing farming, our food system is confronting another problem of our own making: declining insect populations. Insects are agriculture's most under-appreciated labourers. Bees, beetles, ants, moths and butterflies do a serious amount of the legwork when it comes to pollinating fruit trees, vegetable plants and other crops such as cocoa and coffee. According to the Food and Agriculture Organization of the United Nations, the value of crops that rely directly on pollinators is between £177 and £437 billion each year, and rising.[10] But we may not be able to rely on insects to do all this heavy lifting for much longer.

Wherever you look, insect numbers are dropping. One German study stretching over 27 years and 63 nature reserves found that the overall abundance of flying insects fell by 75 per cent between 1989 and 2016.[11] In the US the once-ubiquitous rusty patched bumble bee is now on the brink of extinction after populations fell by nearly 90 per cent in the last 20 years, while researchers in the Netherlands estimated that butterfly populations in the country declined by 84 per cent in the last 130 years.[12] Insects might be the main victims of what biologists have called the 'sixth mass extinction' – a dramatic drop in animal biodiversity, caused by deliberate and accidental human interference in animal ecosystems. A 2018 headline in the *New York Times Magazine* spelled out the situation in even blunter terms: 'The Insect Apocalypse Is Here'.

Farming is one of the major factors behind falling insect populations. Pulling out hedgerows and trees in order to cram in more wheat fields takes away precious insect habitats. At the same time these vast monocultures – stretches of land where only one kind of plant is grown

– are a boon for pest species that would never normally come across such bountiful food reserves. To a grain aphid, a field of wheat swaying in France's Centre-Val de Loire is an endless buffet composed solely of its favourite dish. The only limiting factor is its appetite. To counteract this problem, farmers turn to insecticides to wipe out the troublesome bugs, but this leads to more difficulties. Some insecticides accumulate in the environment and end up being consumed by bees, killing them outright or interfering with the fertility of male bees. Research has also indicated that pesticides may be responsible for colony collapse disorder, a phenomenon where adult honey bees disappear altogether, leaving behind their food stores and young in mysteriously empty hives.[13]

In 2013 the European Union halted the use of three particularly troublesome pesticides in crops that are attractive to honey bees and other pollinating insects. Five years later it extended the ban to all field crops. But this puts a tiny dent in the pesticide market, which was valued at £11 billion in 2018 and is forecast to grow by 5 per cent per year until 2024. As with herbicide-resistant weeds, the enduring use of pesticides leads to its own problems: more than 500 insect species have some level of pesticide resistance. Perhaps fighting nature with chemicals can only take us so far. If we want a longer-term solution, we might need to get familiar with using bugs to our advantage.

Since the Bronze Age, farmers in what is now the UK have left thin lines of trees to demarcate the border between neighbouring fields. These hedgerows weren't just a useful dividing line, but also came with the added bonus of providing a home for beneficial insects that could pollinate crops and prey on pests – something farmers are in need of today. A study in California's Sacramento Valley found that there were fewer crop-nibbling aphids in fields close to hedgerows, and those same fields were less likely to require insecticide than fields without hedgerows nearby.[14] 'We have to go way, way backwards, not forward, to sort this stuff out,' says Brian Spencer, president of Applied Bio-Nomics, a Canadian company that sells 12 different insects to control pest populations in crops, a technique known as biocontrol. One of Spencer's best-selling insects is a midge called *Aphidoletes aphidimyza*, which has a voracious appetite for aphids when it is in its larval form. In a normal year Spencer grows about 20 million *Aphidoletes* and sells them to pecan and apple-tree growers, who must release a new batch of midges into their crop every five years or so. At Rothamsted Research, a UK agricultural science centre, scientists are investigating whether a parasitic wasp could be useful for combating pests in rapeseed that are mostly resistant to commonly used pesticides.

The majority of Spencer's insects end up being used in greenhouses, flower fields and fruit farms, where lots of high-value crops are grown together in relatively small spaces. But bringing biocontrol to open fields means mimicking hedgerows that can host beneficial insects. 'It's about finding out the optimum blend of thickets and brushes and dedicating maybe ten per cent of your field area for these conservational clusters,' Spencer says. The future of biological control will also depend on finding the right insects to defend against the most troublesome pests. Sourcing beneficial insects is an extremely intricate process – researchers must isolate a predator for a specific pest, test its effectiveness at removing the pests and then make sure that introducing the new insect won't have any unexpected side-effects. Although there are a handful of places like Rothamsted Research that are investigating new biocontrols, the overall market is still tiny compared to pesticides.

For the Swiss entomologist Han Herren, biocontrol is only one step on the path to a new way of thinking about food. Herren's not-for-profit Biovision Foundation is currently running a series of organic farming projects in sub-Saharan Africa that incorporate biocontrol as a way of maintaining yields without having to resort to pesticides. At the core of Herren's philosophy is the idea that we should stop thinking about how much food we can squeeze out of each hectare of land, and start thinking about the best way to manage the land in the long term. He's worried that our current dependence on fertiliser, herbicides and pesticides might have solved the problem of producing enough food, but is leading us down the road towards depleted soil and decimated ecosystems. 'If you look at one side, just kilograms per hectare, we've done well,' he says. 'But what [we] did was exploit natural resources rather than manage them.'

In the right circumstances, smarter farms with robotic helpers, recycled water and insecticide-free pest control can all help to reduce the environmental impact of farming, but it might be even better if we can stop farms going down the environmentally damaging route in the first place. In parts of the world like sub-Saharan Africa, where herbicide and artificial fertiliser use is already much lower than in the rest of the world, projects like Herren's are helping farmers skip past the most environmentally damaging forms of farming in favour of a more sustainable approach. As farmers continue to walk the fine line between productivity and sustainability they will need to combine new technology with age-old farming techniques to find a way to reduce the impact our food has on the environment.

4

Unlocking the oceans' potential

The life of an Atlantic salmon is one long, gruelling road trip. Born in coastal rivers in Europe, North America, Iceland and Russia, once the young salmon hit adolescence they head out of their natal waters to the frigid North Atlantic, where they gorge themselves on squid and krill. Once they have built up their energy reserves, the salmon use the Earth's magnetic field and their finely honed sense of smell to find their way back upstream to the exact same riverbed they were born in, where they spawn the next generation of salmon. By the end of this journey, which can cover several thousand kilometres, the fish are so exhausted that many of them perish. A couple of years later the next generation of salmon will be old enough to start the cycle all over again. You're born, you swim thousands of kilometres, you die.

But inside a sprawling white-panelled factory on a sun-baked former tomato field south of Miami there are hundreds of thousands of Atlantic salmon leading lives that would leave their wild relatives utterly baffled. These salmon are born indoors and die indoors, spending their lives cycling between a series of vast circular tanks that together hold more than 60 million litres of water. Some of the tanks are filled with freshwater, to mimic rivers, while others contain seawater drawn from the Atlantic Ocean, which lies 24 kilometres to the east of the building. According to Thue Holm, chief technology officer of Atlantic Sapphire – the Norwegian firm building the plant – by the end of 2022 the facility located in Homestead, Florida, will be able to produce approximately 10,000 tonnes of salmon a year. When it is completed it will fulfil a sizeable chunk of the US demand for fresh salmon.

As you might expect from one of the people behind the world's biggest experiment in land-based fish farming, Holm is convinced that the future of food lies in the oceans. He might have a point. Oceans cover 71 per cent of the planet's surface, but at present provide us with only about 2 per cent of our total food and around 15 per cent of all the animal protein consumed by humans.[1] According to the EAT-*Lancet* report – a wide-ranging study that attempted to pinpoint what the best kind of diet would look like, in terms of the planet's health and our own – seafood is the one source of animal protein that we should be eating more of. The report estimated that a global shift to a 'planetary health diet' that emphasises fruits, vegetables, nuts and wholegrains would also require more than double the current levels of fish production.

Fish aren't simply a much healthier source of protein; they have a relatively small impact on the environment too. Compared to most land animals, the Atlantic salmon swimming in Holm's farm are remarkably efficient machines. Since they are cold-blooded and are supported by the buoyancy of water, fish can channel more of their energy into growth, which means they need fewer calories from food than other livestock. It takes about 1.15 kilograms of fish feed to produce a kilogram of farmed salmon – significantly lower than any commonly farmed land animal. It's the same basic reason why companies like Upside Foods are opting to grow beef in bioreactors: more efficient methods of meat production should come with lower greenhouse-gas emissions. In a world of 9.7 billion people in need of a nutritious, readily available and sustainable source of protein, fish look like one of our best bets.

So where are all these fish going to come from? Not the open ocean, where almost 60 per cent of widely eaten fish are already being fished at their maximally sustainable limits.[2] Wild-capture fishing has chipped away at the ocean's fish populations, leaving many species badly depleted. In the United States, salmon used to be found in almost every single coastal river northeast of New York's Hudson, but now the country's only remaining wild populations occupy a handful of rivers in Maine.[3] The same story repeats itself almost wherever you look in the water. In 2010 the total mass of Pacific bluefin tuna capable of breeding reached its lowest-ever recorded level – just 11 per cent of its 1952 numbers. In 2015 the World Wildlife Fund released a report revealing that overfishing, habitat destruction and climate change had caused fish populations to fall by nearly half between 1970 and 2012.[4] The oceans aren't able to meet our current demand for fish, let alone feed future generations.

'Hunting and gathering out of the ocean is a joke. We haven't hunted and gathered for most of our food on land for three thousand years,' says Kevin Fitzsimmons at the University of Arizona's College of Agriculture and Life Sciences. The alternative, to Fitzsimmons, is obvious. Rather than pluck fish out of the sea, why not repeat what we already do with livestock and crops: grow them intensively at scale? Globally fishing has been heading in this direction for decades. In 1961 farmed fish made up about 5 per cent of the world's entire seafood production, but since the late 1980s fish farming, also known as aquaculture, has boomed. In most aquaculture, farmed fish are kept in net pens – large circular cages usually made from steel or plastic, anchored to the ocean floor or the bottom of freshwater ponds or lakes. In 2013 the volume of seafood produced in this way overtook wild capture for the first time, and since then the gap has continued to grow. Since the mid-1990s the world's total production of wild-caught fish has plateaued, while the amount of fish coming from farms has more than tripled. The aquaculture industry has grown up exceptionally fast. 'What we did with terrestrial agriculture in three thousand years we have done in aquaculture essentially in the last thirty,' says Fitzsimmons.

But if the history of farming has taught us anything, it is that intensifying livestock production comes with major drawbacks. In Asia vast stretches of mangrove forest have been cleared to make way for shrimp farms, leaving coastlines more vulnerable to erosion and removing a vital carbon sink. Moreover, keeping so many fish in close proximity concentrates pollution in the form of uneaten food, waste and dead fish. This then leaks into nearby waters, disrupting the delicate ocean ecosystems. Cramped net pens are also a perfect breeding ground for diseases and pests, and there is the extra danger that disease endemic in farmed fish could spill over into wild populations. In 2012 salmon farms in Scotland lost nearly 10 per cent of their total production to amoebic gill disease and other infections that raced through net pens, killing more than 8.5 million fish.[5] In August 2019 Denmark's environmental minister deemed offshore aquaculture so environmentally risky that she called a halt to all new fish farms in the area and prevented existing farms from expanding.

Many fear that net pens will end up becoming the cattle feedlots of the ocean – pollution-generating floating factories whose only aim is to churn out cheap meat at terrific scale. 'We have made some of those mistakes. Stuff we should have learned from terrestrial agriculture that we had to relearn in some cases,' admits Fitzsimmons. But the industry is still in its infancy, and aquaculture farmers are eager to prove that they are the go-to model for efficient and sustainable food production. The race to fix aquaculture will require rethinking which fish we put in net pens, what we feed them and how the farms operate. And for Thue Holm, it all starts with taking the fish out of the ocean altogether.

Fish out of water

There are a few reasons why it might make sense to grow Atlantic salmon thousands of kilometres away from their natural home in the Norwegian fjords, which are still the centre of the 2.5-million-tonne-a-year salmon-farming industry. Growing fish closer to the people who eat it cuts down on transport costs; farming on land reduces the amount of pollution sent directly into the water; and there is no chance that the salmon will escape through a rip in the net and return to the sea. But there is another factor that pushed Atlantic Sapphire halfway across the globe to south Florida: sea lice.

Sea lice are the scourge of the salmon aquaculture industry. The tiny crustaceans hook onto the fish's scales and feed off its skin and blood to survive. In the wild, a salmon can shrug off one or two sea lice without much fuss, but a fully grown female salmon louse can produce more than 1,500 eggs in its lifetime and, in the densely packed environment of a net pen, populations quickly spiral out of control. A dozen sea lice can kill a salmon; smaller infections leave fishes with bright-pink patches of raw flesh around their gills, rendering the fish completely unmarketable. As a result, these pernicious parasites cost the salmon aquaculture industry about £400 million a year.[6] In an effort to keep sea-lice numbers down, salmon farmers have tried bathing salmon in hydrogen peroxide and supplementing net pens with cleaner fish such as wrasse, which happily nibble away at the parasites. In Norway a start-up called Stingray Marine Solutions markets a sea-lice-zapping robot that kills the crustaceans by hitting them with short bursts of light that are harmless to the fish. The technology is currently being used in more than 150 Norwegian salmon pens.

Another potential solution to the sea-lice conundrum is to farm fish in tanks on land. 'All of the biological challenges you have in the sea, you can avoid [on land],' says Atlantic Sapphire's Thue Holm. No diseases brought in by wild fish (or transmitted by farmed fish to the wild), no algal blooms poisoning fish, and no sea lice. 'We don't vaccinate our fish. We don't ever use any antibiotics. And it's impossible for sea lice to survive in our system,' states Holm. In 2011 Atlantic Sapphire's co-founders, Johan Andreassen and Bjorn-Vegard Lovik, partnered with Holm to build their first land-based salmon farm in a small Danish town called Hvide Sande. It now produces 2,400 tonnes of salmon every year. With its Florida farm, Atlantic Sapphire is attempting to take the blueprint of their Danish farm, scale it up and place it right on the doorstep of the nation that consumes more Atlantic salmon than anywhere else in the world.

Atlantic Sapphire settled on Homestead, Florida, because of the location's unique geography. Since salmon start their lives in freshwater before migrating out to sea, land-based farms need to have access to both seawater and freshwater for the fish to grow in. South Florida happens to sit atop ample stores of both: the Biscayne Aquifer provides the region with its freshwater while parts of the Floridan Aquifer are filled with salt water. The Homestead farm draws water from both of these sources to fill its tanks and then pumps the waste water into the boulder zone – a layer of permeable rock that connects to the Atlantic. Over thousands of years, that water will gradually filter through the rock and head back to the ocean.

This elaborate set-up is crucial to mimicking the salmon's natural lifecycle. The farm buys salmon eggs, which are kept in cool, dark conditions until they hatch and the baby fish are transferred to a freshwater tank until they reach 100 grams. At that point, farm technicians simulate winter by turning down the lights for most of the day and the fish are moved from the freshwater tanks into salt-water units, eventually passing through ten different systems in their lifetimes. After 20 months the fully grown fish are piped from their final tank into the farm's processing facility to be stunned, gutted, graded for quality and packaged, ready to be loaded onto trucks. Throughout the entire process, from hatching to their unceremonious entrance into the processing area, the fish never get a single glimpse of the outside world.

But keeping fish in such tightly controlled environments is fraught with technical challenges. Water in the tanks must be circulated, to keep the fish swimming against the current; oxygen must be pumped in, so they can breathe, and waste filtered out to stop the water becoming toxic. If something goes wrong, thanks to a faulty pump or a dodgy sensor, you could have a disaster on your hands. In February 2020 unusually high nitrogen levels killed off 227,000 salmon in Atlantic Sapphire's Danish farm.[7] Four months later the company was forced to harvest 200,000 salmon from its Homestead farm before they were ready, after construction work near a tank distressed the fish.[8] Despite these risks, the Homestead farm is just one of at least 20 different land-based fish farms currently in operation or being built in 11 different countries by various firms.

Not everyone in the industry is convinced that land-based farms are the future of fish production, however. 'It's kind of extraordinary that such a large amount of investment capital is going into these projects when there is no really successful working example of a large-scale [land-based] Atlantic salmon farm,' says Josh Goldman, a man who has spent more than 30 years trying to find a better way to farm fish. Despite his scepticism about the viability of land-based salmon farming, Goldman has been experimenting with the technology longer than almost anyone in the business. In 1990 he opened an indoor fish farm on the banks of the Connecticut River, close to a village called Turners Falls in western Massachusetts. Still in operation today under different owners, it is one of the world's largest and longest continuously running indoor fish farms.

Goldman's obsession with fish farming started when he was in high school reading Frances Moore Lappé's 1971 book *Diet for a Small Planet* – one of the first popular books to emphasise the link between our culinary choices and the environment. A few years later Goldman built a farm with fish and vegetables growing alongside each other (an approach called aquaponics), close to his student dorm at Hampshire College in Amherst, Massachusetts. Years after graduating, he wound up starting companies that farmed tilapia and striped bass, selling the finished product to a group of Chinese restaurant owners who were after a steady stream of fresh, locally sourced fish.

While the Chinese-restaurant gig paid the bills, Goldman had a much bigger plan in mind. He looked at what most fish farmers were producing and saw that the industry was full of compromises. Some fish we farmed because we were already accustomed to eating them, others were cheap and easy to grow in pens. But the ocean is bursting with diversity. There are an estimated 30,000 fish species alone. Surely there was a better fish out there for farming? In 2000 Goldman set out on the hunt for the perfect farmed fish: one that could be easily domesticated, had a low environmental footprint and was so delicious that people would come back for more after they had tried it. For three years he trawled the world in search of a better fish. He raised 30 different species, selling the excess fish to the Chinese restaurant owners, before he hit upon his perfect catch: barramundi, a fish found widely in the Pacific, but rarely eaten outside Australia and South Asia. In 2004 he co-founded a company, Australis Aquaculture, and started farming barramundi in Turners Falls.

Barramundi ticked all of Goldman's boxes. 'It's really been built for farming in a very cool way,' he says. The fish are fast-growing, lay eggs frequently and have large gills, which mean they thrive in low-oxygen environments. Their largely vegetarian diet also cuts down their environmental impact. And they happen to taste good, too: sweet and buttery, with a flaky texture like sea bass. Goldman became barramundi's biggest proselytiser: convincing high-end chefs to start cooking with the fish, and nudging retailers to market it as a healthy, sustainable source of protein. Soon he was fielding calls from big supermarkets wanting to stock as much of his barramundi as they could get their hands on.

As the popularity of his barramundi grew, Goldman began to realise that his indoor farm could only take him so far. To keep his fish healthy, the water in each of his 500,000-litre tanks had to be recycled twice every hour, and the Turners Falls plant had ten of them, plus 35 smaller tanks. On top of that, each tank needed to be topped up with a significant amount of freshwater each day. All this water hauling makes indoor fish farms huge energy hogs. According to one analysis, fresh salmon produced in an indoor farm in the US has double the carbon footprint of salmon produced in a Norwegian net pen.[9] When Goldman ran the numbers he realised that it would cost him twice as much to grow his barramundi indoors in the US as in a net pen in South-East Asia. So in 2006 he found a site much closer to his barramundi's natural habitat: the tropical waters of Van Phong Bay in central Vietnam.

'I realised that this was a place where we could really execute a model that's going to work for this fish,' Goldman says. Today he has more than 60 net pens in the area, with the largest each holding about 150,000 fish – much bigger than his tanks at Turners Falls. Although he never set out to be a large net-pen farmer, Goldman states that intensifying production in the fish's natural habitat makes more environmental sense than endlessly expanding land-based farms. 'If we want to preserve the natural world and restore ecosystems and manage carbon, in some ways, intensification and efficiency are really the smart play so that more natural systems can be returned to non-farming uses.' As long as net pens are built and maintained with the local environment in mind, they don't have to become an ecological burden, he says.

Goldman is also trying to do for the ocean what Small Robot Company is doing for fields: using data to reduce the overall resource footprint of the farm. When the barramundi are being fed, farm technicians watch live camera footage from inside the net to ensure that no feed is falling past the fish. As soon as it looks as if the fish are leaving the pellets, they stop feeding them. Each of the nets is also only farmed for a maximum of a year before being moved, to give the ocean floor time to recover from the pollution the pens release into the water. 'You don't ever let it get to a tipping point,' Goldman says.

Another way to reduce the environmental impact is to grow seaweed alongside the fish. When the nets in Vietnam aren't being used for fish, Goldman experiments with using them to grow seaweed that can be turned into a thickener for milkshakes, yoghurts and ice cream. When seaweed grows, it takes in the nitrogen and phosphorus released from fish waste, balancing out some of the impact of the net pens and also releasing oxygen back into the water. Off the coast of Connecticut a start-up called Greenwave is growing seaweed alongside scallops, mussels, oysters and clams in ocean farms where nutrients are cycled directly between the growing organisms, with no need for external inputs. In Vietnam, Goldman is also hoping that his seaweed could have a big impact elsewhere in the food chain. Through a spin-off project called Greener Grazing, he's growing a type of seaweed called *Asparagopsis*, which has been shown to dramatically slash methane emissions from cattle when added to their diets in small amounts.[10] Greener Grazing has already established a seedbank of different *Asparagopsis* varieties and is currently working out where the best place to grow the seaweed is, and how it could be combined with aquaculture to close the resource loop in fish farming.

No matter how much seaweed you add to a fish farm, it doesn't solve the problem of what to feed them. One of the awkward ironies of the aquaculture industry is that its existence hinges on fish taken from the ocean. Between 1950 and 2010 more than a quarter of all fish caught in the wild weren't destined for our dinner plates at all. Instead they were turned into fishmeal or fish oil, the majority of which goes towards feeding farmed fish.[11] Estimates put the proportion of wild-caught fish that end up going towards fish farms at closer to 12 per cent today, which still adds up to millions of tonnes of fish every year that are taken out of the ocean, only to be fed to farmed fish elsewhere in the world. Most of these fish are small forage species that do the vital grunt work of the ocean: feeding on plankton right at the bottom of the ocean food chain and channelling that energy all the way up to marine predators such as tuna, sea bass and dolphins. But for the aquaculture industry, these fish are a vital source of the protein and fish oil that their farmed fish and shrimp need in order to grow and survive. Without wild-caught fish, the aquaculture industry would be literally dead in the water.

People in aquaculture have known for years that their reliance on wild-caught fish isn't the best look for an industry whose very existence is partly due to the environmental costs of dredging our oceans to fill stomachs. In 2015 Kevin Fitzsimmons from the University of Arizona helped set up the inaugural Fish-Free Feed

Challenge, which, in its latest iteration, offers a $70,000 (£53,000) prize to the three teams that can sell the greatest amount of fish-free feed to salmon, shrimp and other carnivorous-fish farms. In Van Phong Bay the fishmeal fed to Josh Goldman's barramundi is produced from bycatch – unwanted fish accidentally caught by fisherpeople – but he's on a constant mission to improve what he's feeding his fish. Each year he conducts between five and ten different feed trials, tweaking the formulation of his feed to see how it affects fish growth.

A better fish food

Another answer to the fishmeal problem might lie in a vertical farm nestled in the French wine-growing region of Burgundy. There Antoine Hubert runs a farm that specialises in just one crop: mealworms. Inside, the blocky 3,000-square-metre building is stacked high with trays of writhing mealworms, the larvae of the

Tenebrio molitor beetle, half of which will go towards replacing fishmeal in fish feed, with the other half being used in pet food. Currently the farm produces about 1,000 tonnes of product per year, but this is just a testing ground for a much larger facility currently under construction in Amiens in northern France. By the time it is up-and-running in late 2021, Hubert, who is the co-founder of the insect-farming start-up Ÿnsect, expects the farm will be able to produce 100,000 tonnes of mealworm-based products every year.

From an insect farmer's perspective, mealworms are an unusually useful animal. The bugs feed happily on crop waste from wheat, barley or potato farms and processing plants and, unlike grasshoppers – another much-touted source of animal protein – they don't make a habit of jumping out of the trays they live in. After about two months growing in their trays in the largely automated factory the mealworms are steamed to death, sterilised, mechanically crushed and turned into protein meal and insect oil destined for use in animal feed. The manure they produce doesn't go to waste, either. It can be turned into nutrient-packed fertiliser that makes it an attractive replacement or supplement to existing agricultural fertilisers. In summer 2020 Ÿnsect became the first company in the world to obtain marketing approval for an insect-based fertiliser, which Hubert says will soon be sold in garden centres across France.

'Everything that goes in comes out into one of these three products,' says Hubert – manure, insect protein and insect oil. As well as helping fish farmers cut down their carbon footprints (Hubert hopes that his Amiens plant will be certified carbon negative), it looks as though fish feed containing mealworm might help fish grow even more quickly than conventional fish feed. One research group found that after six weeks shrimp that had been fed varying amounts of mealworm had put on more weight than shrimp that had eaten a diet supplemented only with fishmeal.[12] Another study that involved replacing fishmeal with mealworm for sea bream also saw increased fish growth. Some of Ÿnsect's current customers have now completely replaced fishmeal with mealworm, while others use a mix of the two.

For Hubert, fish feed is just the beginning. The animal-feed market is huge – about 1.1 billion tonnes every year – and mealworms could make an attractive supplement for pig and poultry diets, too. His next step is to try and breed even better mealworms with increased protein content or extra minerals. 'Now we're going to start comparing different strains of this *molitor* beetle,' he says. 'We think we can do something interesting by maybe crossing different strands together and highlighting some genetic characteristics.'

But while mealworms and other alternative protein sources like bacteria and algae might help supplant aquaculture's dependence on wild-caught fish, not everyone is convinced aquaculture should be the future source of our seafood.

'The system itself is flawed,' says Marianne Cufone, an environmental lawyer and executive director of the Recirculating Farms Coalition, a group that advocates for small-scale community-based food production. 'What challenges are we causing in trying to ramp up industrial food production? I think there are just a lot of questions there that are not so easily answered.' Cufone is one of the advocates leading the opposition to a planned open-water fish farm in the Gulf of Mexico. In aquaculture terms, the proposed farm is small – just 20,000 Almaco jack fish in a net pen 113 kilometres south-west of Florida – but the decision to go ahead with it or not will have big implications for the future of aquaculture in the United States.

The US is a tiny player when it comes to aquaculture; in fact it imports 85 per cent of all its seafood. Oysters and clams make up the lion's share of its small aquaculture industry, with salmon, mussels and shrimp lagging way behind. Up until now almost all of this aquaculture has taken place in state-controlled waters, within five kilometres of the coastline, but federal waters, which extend between five and 320 kilometres from the coast-line, represent a hitherto-untapped source of open space that could be filled with fish farms. And it looks like the

US could be opening up to open-ocean aquaculture in its waters. In August 2019 the US Environmental Protection Agency issued a draft permit for the Almaco jack farm in the Gulf of Mexico to Ocean Era, a Hawaii-based aquaculture firm that has already conducted two open-ocean trials in the waters near Hawaii.

In May 2020 the Trump administration signed an executive order pushing federal authorities to prioritise open-ocean aquaculture. Three months later the National Oceanic and Atmospheric Administration (NOAA) officially designated the Gulf of Mexico and waters off southern California as the country's first 'Aquaculture Opportunity Areas', which are earmarked for between three and five commercial aquaculture farms. The main driver behind the Trump administration's push for aquaculture was a desire to make the country more food-secure, but as critics of the move point out, America already exports about 84 per cent of its domestically caught fish, some of which eventually returns to the country as imports.

Opponents to open-ocean aquaculture in the United States argue that big fish farms will damage coastal fishing communities and won't help people who really need access to cheap, healthy sources of protein. 'When it comes to food access, much of that fish doesn't end up on the plates of those who need the food most,' says Niaz Dorry, coordinating director at the Northwest Atlantic Marine Alliance, a fisherpeople-led advocacy group. Instead of focusing on fish farms that produce only a handful of species, we should be eating a much wider range of fish that can be fished sustainably by local communities that depend upon the industry, she says.

In August 2020 the push for open-ocean agriculture in the US was dealt a blow when a court ruled that NOAA lacked the authority to designate Aquaculture Opportunity Areas, with the debate likely to continue on Capitol Hill. But for Cufone, the looming threat of fish farms is just another symptom of a country where people are too often disconnected from where their food originates – a problem that goes way beyond fishing.

'What I would love to see is a series of small, local farms producing food for their own communities,' says Cufone. In the Central City neighbourhood of New Orleans she's built a small aquaponic farm fuelled mostly by solar power and rainwater, which farms catfish alongside greens, tomatoes, cucumbers and melons. In the past the farm has sold the fish to local restaurants, and bags of fruit and vegetables to local residents. 'We live in a very low-income area and one of the primary focuses for the farm was to provide food for very low-income, low-resource residents,' she says. 'There's something to be said for community awareness, understanding how hard it is to grow food and understanding the real value of farms and farmers.'

If the world heeds the call for healthier, more sustainable diets, then the way we produce fish is set to become one of the defining issues of the future of food. From where we are now, two things are clear. First, the share of fish that are caught from the wild is likely to keep declining as the aquaculture industry continues to boom. Second, the aquaculture industry is in for a slow reckoning, as companies and governments grapple with the environmental impacts of farming fish. There are plenty of signs, however, that the industry is learning at least some of the lessons from the livestock industry and the environmental chaos it unleashed as it rapidly industrialised. Innovators like Goldman, Fitzsimmons and Hubert are already laying the foundations for a future where animal protein doesn't need to come with such a high environmental cost.

5

Waging war on waste

When the Covid-19 pandemic hit in early 2020 the world's food-supply chains melted into disarray. In Florida the closure of restaurants, schools, theme parks and cruise ships left vegetable farmers with nowhere to send their rapidly ripening produce. In desperation they were forced to plough cucumbers, squash and tomatoes back into the ground. As flights across the globe were cancelled, fruit farmers in the UK warned that without their annual workforce of Eastern European fruit pickers up to one-third of their entire crop would be left in the field.

Meanwhile, as food was rotting in the fields, more people than ever were going hungry. In England, Wales and Northern Ireland food insecurity doubled as the pandemic unfolded, with one in ten people reporting in June that they had to go to a food bank.[1] As with any crisis, the fallout will disproportionately impact the people who are already the most vulnerable. According to figures from the Food and Agriculture Organization of the United Nations (FAO), the economic impact of Covid-19 could push at least another 83 million people worldwide into hunger. The pandemic has thrown into sharp relief what might be the biggest problem facing the world's food systems. Each year around one-third of the planet's entire food production never makes it to our mouths. Food wasted by consumers in developed countries alone adds up to 220 million tonnes per year – almost as much as the entire annual food production of sub-Saharan Africa. As already mentioned, there are an estimated 746 million people who regularly go hungry in the world. In addition there are two billion who don't get the right vitamins and minerals in their diet, yet every day we throw away mountains of edible, nutritious food.

And it's not just the immorality of seeing people starve amid plenty. All this uneaten food also leaves behind a huge environmental footprint. If global food waste was a country, its greenhouse-gas emissions would be third behind only China and the USA. The water alone used to produce this food would fill Lake Geneva three times over, and the land used would cover the whole of Canada and India combined. Eliminating food waste altogether could significantly close the gap between food production and a rapidly growing global population without extending our burden on the planet at the same time.

But there is no silver bullet when it comes to food waste on a global level. Each nation faces wildly different challenges. To work out how we might start to tackle this huge problem, it's helpful to know a little bit of food-waste jargon. Roughly speaking, all wasted food can be divided into two broad categories. Food that is wasted during production, processing or distribution is classed as 'food loss'. Food that is wasted by retailers, food service providers or consumers is chunked together as 'food waste'. This wonkish distinction is important, because the kind of intervention that might help a farmer in Kenya from losing half of their crop to a maize-weevil infestation wouldn't be much help to a restaurant in London that throws away one-third of its steak dinners on any given night. In the former example, cutting down food loss might make the difference between the farmer being able to afford to eat for the rest of the year or not. The steaks, on the other hand, while not being the difference between life and death, probably had a much bigger impact on the environment. When it comes to waste, it's not sufficient merely to ask how much is being wasted; the only way we can start to come up with solutions is to work out what is being wasted, why and by whom.

Cutting food loss

Rosa Rolle's job is to find the answers to these questions. A team leader at the FAO's Food and Nutrition Division, she's a food-waste detective, tasked with travelling to countries in the developing world, working out where food is being lost and finding ways to stop it happening.

Her starting point is usually the local market. 'This is where you have the highest levels of losses, and these are the markets that really feed the local people,' she says. On one such trip to Laos she remembers seeing trucks of tomatoes where entire truckbeds were covered with inedible crushed tomatoes. 'You could just see the tomato juice falling out of the trucks,' she says. This wasn't an isolated incident – one study from Odisha state in India found that around one-third of tomatoes were lost after they had been harvested, most while they were being transported to urban markets.[2]

But small changes can make a huge difference. During one project in Bangladesh, Rolle asked farmers to swap the plastic mesh sacks they normally used to transport tomatoes for smaller plastic crates. As a result the number of tomatoes surviving the journey from farm to market skyrocketed. When they were using the large sacks, a little over half of the fruit was still salvageable by the time it reached the market. With the crates, almost 95 per cent of the fruit made it. 'This helps to tremendously reduce the level of losses, and then you have better fruit going into the market. So at the end of the day, everyone in that supply chain began to benefit as a result,' says Rolle. If the tomatoes arrive in better condition, they last longer on the shelf and retailers don't have to pass on the cost of the wasted tomatoes to consumers; plus the people buying the tomatoes benefit because they have easier access to nutritious food. 'People begin to see these benefits, they realise them in terms of their incomes, so they're very quick to take [the crates] up,' says Rolle.

West and Central Africa are facing an entirely different food-loss problem. One of the region's most important crops is cowpea, a protein-rich legume that is a key source of protein, particularly for rural communities. Unfortunately the cowpea weevil also has an appetite for these nutritious beans, and the pests can easily destroy entire bags of stored cowpea within two or three months. Because of this, cowpea farmers are forced to make an unenviable decision after every harvest. Either they sell their crop when the markets are already flooded with cowpea and prices are low, or they take the risk of storing their harvest, in the hope that enough of the crop will survive to be sold when prices pick up again after a few months. Many farmers, under pressure to make money to pay for food and school fees, are forced to sell their crop when prices are at rock bottom, rather than take a gamble on storage.

But a relatively simple solution is turning this situation around. In 1987 an American entomologist called Larry Murdock was part of a team investigating beetle infestations in Cameroon when he hit upon the idea of storing cowpea in triple-layered airtight bags that starve any lurking weevils of oxygen, eventually killing them altogether. Cowpea stored in these bags, instead of the conventional woven bags, barely showed any signs of infestation after five months.[3] Murdock set about trying to generate interest in his bags, which he called Purdue Improved Crop Storage (PICS), eventually receiving an $11.8 million (£8.9 million) grant from the Bill & Melinda

Gates Foundation to start selling them in West and Central Africa. As of 2020, 25 million PICS bags have been sold in at least 35 countries, adding an estimated $1.8 billion (£1.34 billion) in revenue to farmers, who can now hang on to more of their cowpea and sell it when prices are higher.

Limiting food waste after storage also decreases the environmental footprint of food. Land used to grow cowpea that ended up being wasted could instead be turned into a vegetable patch, or returned to nature. 'We don't have to put more land into production if we can increase the availability of food through better storage,' says Murdock. After a third grant from the Bill & Melinda Gates Foundation, the PICS team is now building a network of manufacturers, distributors and retailers to make the bags as widely available as possible. 'If everyone in the value chain makes a profit, it will sustain itself when we're gone,' says Murdock. 'We can go away and it'll still be there and the benefits will continue.'

Cutting food waste

In a region like sub-Saharan Africa, which is home to a quarter of all the world's undernourished people, food waste is the line between farmers having enough money to feed their family or going hungry.[4] But once food finds its way to consumers, hardly any of it goes to waste – just 4 per cent of the total food wastage in sub-Saharan Africa happens at this point. In more affluent parts of the world, this dynamic is turned dramatically on its head. In Europe more than 30 per cent of the total food wasted is thrown away at the very end of the supply chain, in our restaurants and homes. From an environmental perspective, food wasted at this stage is as bad as it gets, because its carbon footprint includes all the energy it took to grow, store, process, distribute, cook and ultimately dispose of it. On top of that, you have the problem that because people in wealthier countries tend to eat more meat, the environmental footprint of the food they are throwing away is proportionally far higher than in poor countries. Although meat and milk only make up 11 per cent of food wasted, they account for almost 78 per cent of the total land dedicated to producing wasted food. Reducing food waste in our homes and restaurants could be one of the easiest ways in which most people can help lessen the environmental impact of our diets.

In the UK 12 per cent of all food waste takes place in the hospitality industry. A company called Winnow is trying to bring this figure way down. A big commercial kitchen is a lot like a factory, explains Winnow's co-founder Kevin Duffy. At every stage of the production process there are opportunities for wastage. Food is dropped on the floor; the salmon isn't trimmed in the most efficient way; food that was overordered spoils in the fridge; a tray of biscuits goes awry in the oven and has to be disposed of. In most kitchens that Duffy has worked with, this wastage – even before any food has been served to customers – adds up to 5–15 per cent of all the food bought in. Some of the worst offenders waste up to one-fifth of purchased food.

'Any factory that did that wouldn't survive very long, but in the restaurant industry that's just par for the course,' Duffy says. Chefs are pressed for time, they have hungry bellies to fill and are not necessarily paying attention to everything that is ending up in the bin. 'It's not that the kitchens are actually wanting to waste their work [...] but to be careful with food and not waste edible food, you have to be paying attention, you have to be monitoring data.'

Duffy's solution is called Winnow Vision. It combines a digital scale, a tablet computer and a connected camera, pointing down to peer at the contents of a bin below. When a chef adds food to the bin, the Winnow system weighs the food being added, uses machine vision to categorise the food and adds that information to a central database that records exactly what is being wasted, how much of it and when. Businesses can use the data to change what food they order and how they prepare it, and Duffy says that Winnow users tend to reduce their food purchasing costs by 2–8 per cent every year. It's a similar approach to Small Robot Company's per-plant farming – with data, businesses can be more efficient, can waste fewer resources and can target their efforts in the right areas.

Sometimes the recommendations that the Winnow system yields are blindingly obvious, in retrospect. Duffy recalls one high-end hotel kitchen that would start every breakfast service at six in the morning by cooking ten trays of scrambled eggs in one go. By the end of breakfast none of the customers were touching the eggs, because by that point they had been sitting there for four hours. The restaurant was chucking whole trays in the bin every day. Other insights are less obvious: in one corporate canteen the pasties were a top-seller throughout the day, until it came to the evening service. Then, at the same point every weekday, the number of pasties going in the bin would shoot up. It turned out that the chef responsible for cooking the evening pasties had been misreading a recipe and tripling the amount of salt required. 'It's not rocket science,' says Duffy. 'A lot of it is just identifying pretty simple data, root cause, and then giving it to the right people at the right time.' It may not be rocket science, but tracking waste can make a huge impact. The Winnow system has now been used by large hospitality companies such as Hilton, Marriott and Carnival Cruise Line as well as IKEA, which credited Winnow and a US company that makes similar technology with helping the furniture firm save 350,000 meals from being wasted in just eight months.

While restaurants might be able to cut down the food they are throwing away by installing a system like Winnow, ordinary households might find it a little harder to get to grips with their food waste. Homes are the biggest food-waste culprit in the UK by far. More than 70 per cent of all edible food that is wasted after it has left the farm is squandered by households – with restaurants accounting for 12 per cent and retailers just 4 per cent.[5] If we want to really cut down our food waste, we will have to start by looking in our own kitchens.

Tessa Clarke has one solution to this problem. After growing up on a dairy farm in North Yorkshire, she was already in the habit of trying to waste as little food as possible. But it was while moving from Geneva back to the UK in December 2014 that she found the impetus to turn her dislike of food waste into a career. The removal firm packing up Clarke's flat asked her to throw away her leftover food rather than shipping it back to the UK – something she couldn't bring herself to do. She ventured out of her apartment to find someone in need, to give the excess food to, but the streets were empty. She thought about knocking on her neighbours' doors and giving the food to them, but she feared they would find it odd and embarrassing. In tears, she sneaked the non-perishable items in her packing anyway, hoping that the removal firm wouldn't notice. Back in London, Clarke realised that giving away food shouldn't feel awkward or weird. 'What's really weird is wasting food,' she says. So she co-founded a start-up called Olio with her friend Saasha Celestial-One, with the aim of making food sharing a normal part of life.

Olio is a food-sharing app that lets anyone upload a listing of food that would otherwise go to waste and then invite a neighbour to come and pick it up. In April 2015 Clarke tested the idea with a group of 12 strangers living in north London, bringing them together in a WhatsApp group and asking them to share any spare food with their fellow experimenters. Clarke and Celestial-One waited for more than 24 hours before the first share came in: half a bag of shallots. Twenty-three minutes later they were snapped up by a neighbour. 'What I realised is that no one enjoys wasting food, but the reason they do it is because they have no one to give their food to,' says Clarke. 'We've moved away from our families, away from our relatives, away from our friends. We live in these little boxes, we work somewhere different from where we live, so we don't know who our neighbours are. And so for all those reasons, we live like a little atom in our community. We're just not connected to our community any more.'

Clarke launched the first version of the Olio app in July 2015, limited initially to five postcodes in north London. Fifteen months later it was available worldwide. As of November 2020, Olio users have shared eight million portions of food in 53 different countries. Half of the food shared on the platform comes from businesses, which pay to have one of Olio's 10,000 volunteers pick up their excess food at the end of the day, rather than getting a waste contractor to take it to landfill or having it turned into biogas. 'Food waste is starting to be seen as completely unacceptable, for a business to put out on the street a clear bag full of perfectly edible food to be taken off to the trash when it could be redistributed to the local community,' says Clarke. Businesses now using the app include Pret a Manger, Tesco, Eurostar, Costa Coffee and Compass Catering.

When the Covid-19 pandemic took hold in early 2020 and countries started issuing lockdown orders requiring residents to stay indoors, Clarke feared that sharing on Olio would dry up. 'We had a hair-raising 24 to 48 hours when lockdown was announced and it was unclear whether a neighbour-to-neighbour food-sharing app could even continue to exist or not,' she says. But after a slow couple of weeks, use of the app started shooting back up. 'It only takes a few photographs of empty supermarket shelves to be reminded very viscerally of how critical food is.'

According to the waste-reduction charity WRAP, the countrywide lockdown the UK entered in mid-March had a big impact on changing attitudes to food waste. 'We were seeing people undertaking lots of different behaviour during lockdown,' says the company's head of citizen-behaviour change, Sarah Clayton. With restaurants closed and citizens instructed by the government to shop for necessities 'as infrequently as possible', more people started picking up waste-reducing habits, like checking their cupboards before shopping, and storing leftover cooked food to eat later. 'The biggest change we want is for food waste to be socially unacceptable,' says Clayton.

Clark agrees. '[Reducing food waste] is the poor cousin of climate-crisis solutions because it doesn't sound particularly fun or sexy, but the reality is it's one of the most powerful levers for solving the climate crisis,' she says. In 2019 a group of Olio users in south London started a community garden where all the surplus vegetables are shared on the platform. By 2030 – in time for the UN's deadline for halving food waste – she wants one billion people to have used Olio. Just like Marianne Cufone's community farm in central New Orleans, one way to tackle the inefficiencies of our food system is by re-injecting a sense of community into the way we distribute and use food. Although it's tempting to think about the future of food as a problem of supply only, by considering the demand side as well, we can reduce the need to convert more land to farmland and put more resources into the soil.

Conclusion:
Thinking about food

In 2009 the Swedish environmental scientist Johan Rockström and an international team of researchers set out a series of planetary thresholds that humans should not cross. These boundaries defined what they called the 'safe operating space for humanity', and crossing any of them could trigger abrupt and unpredictable changes to the planet that would make it much less liveable for humans. Rockström and his colleagues settled on nine boundaries.[1] Humans must not:

1. Release too much carbon dioxide into the atmosphere
2. Wipe out too many species too quickly
3. Put too much nitrogen and phosphorus from fertiliser into the land

4. Use up too much freshwater

5. Convert too much land to agriculture

6. Make the oceans too acidic

7. Deplete the ozone layer

8. Pump too many aerosols into the atmosphere

9. Dump too many chemicals into the environment.

Four of these boundaries have already been crossed: carbon emissions, species extinction, nitrogen and phosphorus release, and land-use change.

The planetary-boundaries model is not universally adored by climate scientists. Some argue that the list oversimplifies the difference between regional and global problems.[2] Others say that these hard limits don't make it any easier for governments to set policies to keep within these boundaries. But there are a couple of ways in which these nine boundaries provide a useful framework for thinking about the future of food. First, they are a stark reminder that the food we eat has profound impacts on the environment. Farming has a very significant influence on all nine of those planetary boundaries – for several, it is the single biggest contributor. Second, they remind us that we simply can't disconnect the production of our food from the environment it depends on, which means that every tweak we make to our food systems is a trade-off. Want to reduce water usage by switching to high-tech vertical farms? Fine, but be prepared for carbon emissions from energy to go up as a result. Prefer to see a world without artificial fertiliser? Go ahead, but you might have to increase the size of your farm, if you don't want production to drop as a result.

'Every solution brings new problems,' says Tara Garnett, a researcher at the University of Oxford's Environmental Change Institute, who specialises in understanding how food systems contribute to greenhouse-gas emissions. The Green Revolution may have ushered in an era of superweeds and farms that disgorge fertiliser into rivers and oceans, but this phenomenal intensification of farming also saved billions of hectares of land from being converted to farmland. According to some estimates, if we were still farming cereal crops at the kind of yields seen in 1961, we would have to convert an extra 1.26 billion hectares to farmland in order to produce the same amount of food we do today – a swathe of land about the same size as Mexico and Europe combined. We eased off on one planetary boundary only by pushing at another. The same is true when it comes to the future of food. We can't expect the farms of the future to be perfect, but we should carefully weigh up the pros and cons of new ways of producing food, and be prepared to change our mind if our hoped-for salve turns out to have its own problems.

But there is one important aspect of farming that the planetary-boundaries model does not capture: the people involved in making our food. 'We just expect food to be available and everyone wants to pay the least for it,' says Emily Broad Leib, director of Harvard Law School Food Law and Policy Clinic. 'There's a striking lack of realism in terms of what [paying for food] looks like and what the cost of production actually is.' More than one billion people work in the agricultural industry – a little over a quarter of the world's entire working population, and a figure that varies wildly depending on which country you are looking at.[3] In the UK a little over 1 per cent of the entire labour force works in farming, while in Chad it is more than 87 per cent. When we talk about fixing our food systems, whose problems are we really trying to solve? Farmers who rely on government subsidies to eke out a living? People who are undernourished or – as is increasingly the case in parts of the developed world – suffering from overnourishment? Future generations who will face greater climate uncertainty than any who went before them?

A single innovation – no matter how ingenious – can tackle only a small slice of the problems facing the world's food system. Factories growing meat, ultra-precise farming robots and food-sharing apps are all part of a vast patchwork of potential solutions that can nudge us towards a better food system. Armed with what we now know about the impact that our food has on the world, it will come down to all of us – governments, scientists, businesses, farmers and the rest of us – to make better decisions about how we want our food to be grown and distributed. If we can make enough of the right choices, it might just be possible to feed the planet without pushing it beyond its limits.

Acknowledgements

This book could not have been written without the help of many people. I'm extremely grateful to the scientists, activists, farmers and entrepreneurs who generously shared with me their time and expertise. If we can feel optimistic about the future of food and the planet – and I think we can – then it is in no small part thanks to their dedication and imagination.

Many of the people who helped with this book are mentioned within its pages. Others are unnamed, but their contributions were equally important. In no particular order, I wish to thank: Mark Post, Bruce Friedrich, Uma Valeti, Liz Specht, Didier Toubia, Mark Kozubal, Thomas Jonas, Amy Rowat, Krijn de Nood, Daan Luining, Isha Datar, Glenn Gregorio, Hans Bhardwaj, Gilad Gershon, Ofir Meir, Eyal Maori, Abdulai Jalloh, Hannah Wittman, Randy Ploetz, James Dale, Michael Clark, Edo Bar-Zeev,

Andrew Challinor, Richard Ballard, Hans Herren, Clint Brauer, Sam Watson-Jones, Brian Spencer, Tara Garnett, Neil Mattson, Marianne Cufone, Thue Holm, Antoine Hubert, Kevin Fitzsimmons, Josh Goldman, Niaz Dorry, Mike Selden, Benjamin Thomas, Emily Broad Leib, Rosa Rolle, Larry Murdock, Kevin Duffy, David Walker, Sarah Clayton and Tessa Clarke.

As with any work of non-fiction, this book builds on the journalism and scholarship of many remarkable people. The team at Our World in Data – particularly Max Roser and Hannah Ritchie – helped make sense of how far the world has come, and how far we still have to go. The writings of Neil Stephens and Benjamin Wurgaft were indispensable in guiding me through the world of cultivated meat. Books from Nagesh Prabhu, Nick Cullather and Charles Mann helped me understand the politics and pitfalls of the Green Revolution. Dan Koeppel's book on bananas is vital reading for anyone who wants to understand this world-changing fruit. Lastly, the podcast Gastropod by Cynthia Graber and Nicola Twilley was a constant source of information and spurred my curiosity about the world of food. Any readers who find their interest similarly piqued would do well to start there.

A special thanks is due to my colleagues at *WIRED*. Without Greg Williams and Mike Dent this series of books would not exist. James Temperton has been a constant source of encouragement in my reporting, much of which formed the basis for this book. Nigel Wilcockson shaped the book from the very first outline to the final edit, and it is much stronger thanks to his thoughtful approach. My thanks to him and everyone at Penguin. Any mistakes, of course, are mine alone.

This book would not have been possible without the support of Tayla McCloud. Through a difficult pandemic year, and across three cities, her encouragement and insight were unfailing. Thank you.

Notes

Notes to Introduction: A planet at
a crossroads   pages 1–9

1   http://www.fao.org/faostat/en/

2   https://ourworldindata.org/world-population-growth

3   https://www.thelancet.com/journals/lancet/article/
     PIIS0140-6736(15)00480–8/fulltext

4   http://www.fao.org/3/a0750e/a0750e00.htm

5   Other estimates put this figure as high as 92 per cent;
     see Hoekstra, Arjen Y. and Mekonnen, Mesfin M., 2012,
     'The water footprint of humanity', *Proceedings of the
     National Academy of Sciences*, https://doi.org/10.1073/
     pnas.1109936109; and Food and Agriculture Organization
     of the United Nations, 2011, 'The State of the World's
     Land and Water Resources for Food and Agriculture',
     http://www.fao.org/3/i1688e/i1688e00.htm

6   Not everyone agrees with these projections. In July
     2020 a study in the journal *The Lancet* suggested that
     the UN's population projections were overestimating
     the rate of population growth. The authors of the *Lancet*
     study project that the global population will peak at 9.73
     billion in 2064, before declining to 8.79 billion in 2100
     because of falling overall fertility rates. In any case, the
     central dynamic is the same: with populations going up
     and becoming more wealthy, demand on food production
     is set to increase significantly. See Vollset, Stein Emil et
     al., 2020, 'Fertility, mortality, migration, and population
     scenarios for 195 countries and territories from 2017
     to 2100: a forecasting analysis for the Global Burden of
     Disease Study', *The Lancet*, https://doi.org/10.1016/S0140-
     6736(20)30677–2

7   The precise level of food-production increase is disputed.
     Some scientists put the increase needed at between 25
     and 70 per cent of 2017 levels. See Hunter, Mitchell C.
     et al., 2017, 'Agriculture in 2050: Recalibrating targets

for sustainable intensification', *Bioscience*, https://doi.
org/10.1093/biosci/bix010

8   http://www.fao.org/publications/sofi/2020/en/

9   http://www.fao.org/3/mb060e/mb060e.pdf

Notes to 1 Replacing meat   pages 11–42

1   https://science.sciencemag.org/content/360/6392/987

2   http://www.fao.org/3/i3437e/i3437e00.htm

3   Carbon-dioxide equivalents are a way of accounting for
    the fact that greenhouse gases have different impacts on
    global warming. Methane, for example, has around 28–36
    times the warming potential of carbon dioxide over 100
    years. Carbon-dioxide equivalents add all these together
    and express emissions in a single figure, rather than having
    to detail each gas separately.

4   In farming jargon this is called the 'feed conversion ratio',
    and chickens are about the most efficient land-based
    livestock out there. For every two kilograms of feed that a
    chicken eats, it puts on about one kilogram of body weight.

Things are complicated when you consider only the parts of animals eaten as meat, but the general principle holds true: ruminants (cows, sheep and goats) are far less efficient than pigs, poultry and fish.

5   https://www.beefmagazine.com/beef-quality/has-us-become-ground-beef-nation

6   https://www.washingtonpost.com/archive/lifestyle/2000/02/11/pelting-the-pelts/515beb9b-c355-4101-8a33-b11c8c254468/

7   Livestock are routinely fed large quantities of antibiotics to counter bacterial infections that can be endemic in crowded living conditions. This widespread use of antibiotics (up to 80 per cent of medically important antibiotics in some countries go towards livestock) has led to a rise in drug-resistant bacteria that can jump from animals into humans. See Liu, Cindy M. et al., 2018, 'Escherichia coli ST131-H22 as a foodborne uropathogen', mBio, 9 (4), https://mbio.asm.org/content/9/4/e00470-18

8   http://www.fao.org/faostat/en/

9   https://www.pnas.org/content/115/25/6506

10   https://gfi.org/resource/cultivated-meat-eggs-and-dairy-
     state-of-the-industry-report/

11   https://gfi.org/resource/analyzing-cell-culture-medium-
     costs/

12   https://www.nature.com/articles/s43016-020–0046-5

13   https://pubmed.ncbi.nlm.nih.gov/21682287/

14   https://pubmed.ncbi.nlm.nih.gov/26383898/

15   https://www.wsj.com/articles/the-secret-of-these-new-
     veggie-burgers-plant-blood-1412725267

16   https://www.wired.com/story/the-impossible-
     burger/

17   https://impossiblefoods.com/sustainable-food/burger-life-
     cycle-assessment-2019

18   https://www.theguardian.com/business/2019/may/14/
     greggs-vegan-sausage-rolls-fuel-profit-boom

19   https://gfi.org/marketresearch/

Notes to 2 Improving crops   pages 43–69

1   https://idl-bnc-idrc.dspacedirect.org/handle/10625/88

2   https://www.sciencedirect.com/science/article/abs/pii/
    S0378429010002066

3   https://ourworldindata.org/yields-vs-land-use-how-
    has-the-world-produced-enough-food-for-a-growing-
    population

4   https://www.nature.com/articles/ncomms2296

5   https://www.nature.com/articles/s41558-018-0313-8

6   https://cropgeneticsinnovation.ucdavis.edu/new-flood-
    tolerant-rice-offers-relief-worlds-poorest-farmers

7   https://gtr.ukri.org/projects?ref=BB%2FN020847%2F1

8   https://www.nature.com/articles/s41467-017-01670-6

9   https://www.sciencedirect.com/science/article/pii/
    S1931312819303658

10 https://www.nature.com/articles/d41586-019-02770-7

11 https://www.dtnpf.com/agriculture/web/ag/crops/
    article/2019/12/16/grower-sets-new-world-record-corn-2

12 https://openknowledge.worldbank.org/handle/10986/5990

13 https://www.ipcc.ch/report/ar5/wg2/

14 https://www.mdpi.com/2071-1050/12/8/3493

Notes to 3 Reducing farming's footprint   pages 71–96

1   https://enveurope.springeropen.com/articles/10.1186/
    s12302-016-0070-0; https://pubmed.ncbi.nlm.nih.
    gov/31342895/

2   https://www.croplife.com/crop-inputs/historic-prevent-
    planting-in-2019-requires-a-solid-weed-control-plan-this-
    year/

3   https://pubmed.ncbi.nlm.nih.gov/29773742/

4   https://www.nature.com/articles/srep04586

5   https://www.noaa.gov/media-release/large-dead-zone-
    measured-in-gulf-of-mexico

6   https://www.tandfonline.com/doi/
    abs/10.1080/02508060008686794

7   http://www.fao.org/aquastat/en/countries-and-basins/
    country-profiles/country/SAU

8   https://openknowledge.worldbank.org/
    handle/10986/27659

9   https://www.nature.com/articles/s41545-019-0039-9

10 http://www.fao.org/documents/card/en/c/i9527en/

11 https://journals.plos.org/plosone/article?id=10.1371/
journal.pone.0185809

12 https://www.nationalgeographic.com/science/article/
bumblebees-endangered-extinction-united-states

13 https://www.researchgate.net/publication/228522711_In_
situ_replication_of_honey_bee_colony_collapse_disorder

14 https://www.sciencedirect.com/science/article/abs/pii/
S0167880914001662

Notes to 4 Unlocking the oceans' potential   page 97–125

1 https://eatforum.org/learn-and-discover/aquatic-food-
sustainable-healthy-diets/

2 http://www.fao.org/documents/card/en/c/I9540EN/

3 https://www.fisheries.noaa.gov/species/atlantic-salmon-
protected

4 https://assets.wwf.org.uk/downloads/living_blue_planet_
report_2015.pdf

5 https://www.heraldscotland.com/news/13091770.disease-
deaths-on-salmon-farms-soar/

6   https://www.seafoodsource.com/news/aquaculture/the-
    sticky-problem-of-sea-lice-and-what-s-being-done-to-
    stop-them

7   https://www.undercurrentnews.com/2020/03/02/atlantic-
    sapphire-loses-227000-salmon-in-denmark-ras-facility/

8   https://www.seafoodsource.com/news/aquaculture/
    atlantic-sapphire-suffers-mass-salmon-mortality-at-its-
    florida-ras-farm

9   This figure only accounts for the production of the
    fish, not for transport. If that Norwegian salmon is
    then air-freighted to the US (as is often the case), the
    environmental pendulum swings in the other direction and
    the net pen has twice the carbon footprint of the indoor
    farm. Flash-freezing fish and transporting it on cargo ships
    instead dramatically reduces the carbon footprint of any
    fish. See Liu, Yajie et al., 2016, 'Comparative economic
    performance and carbon footprint of two farming models
    for producing Atlantic salmon (*Salmo salar*): Land-based
    closed containment system in freshwater and open net

pen in seawater', *Aquacultural Engineering*, 71, https://doi.org/10.1016/j.aquaeng.2016.01.001

10 https://animalmicrobiome.biomedcentral.com/articles/10.1186/s42523-019-0004-4

11 https://www.researchgate.net/publication/313684262_Most_fish_destined_for_fishmeal_production_are_food-grade_fish

12 https://www.researchgate.net/publication/327667093_Replacing_fish_meal_by_mealworm_Tenebrio_molitor_on_the_growth_performance_and_immunologic_responses_of_white_shrimp_Litopenaeus_vannamei

Notes to 5 Waging war on waste   pages 127–144

1 https://www.theguardian.com/uk-news/2020/aug/12/coronavirus-lockdown-hits-nutritional-health-of-uks-poorest

2 https://worldveg.tind.io/record/31826

3 https://www.researchgate.net/publication/230818871

4 https://datatopics.worldbank.org/sdgatlas/

5   https://wrap.org.uk/resources/report/food-surplus-and-
     waste-uk-key-facts

Notes to Conclusion: Thinking about food   pages 145–150

1   https://www.nature.com/articles/461472a

2   https://pubmed.ncbi.nlm.nih.gov/22622531/

3   https://data.worldbank.org/

Index

WIRED Guides: the must-read series of WIRED books on the key trends and topics shaping our world.

CLIMATE CHANGE
how we can get to carbon zero

BIANCA NOGRADY

WIRED

ARTIFICIAL INTELLIGENCE
how machine learning will shape the next decade

MATT BURGESS

WIRED

THE FUTURE OF MEDICINE
how we will enjoy longer, healthier lives

JAMES TEMPERTON

WIRED

On sale March 2021

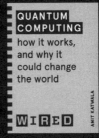

THE FUTURE OF FOOD
how to feed the planet without destroying it

MATT REYNOLDS

WIRED

QUANTUM COMPUTING
how it works, and why it could change the world

AMIT KATWALA

WIRED

CRYPTO CURRENCY
how digital money could transform finance

GIAN VOLPICELLI

WIRED

On sale from June 2021

WIRED Consulting takes
the **WIRED** knowledge,
network and brand to our
clients, helping them
to drive innovation, shape
strategy and build their
voice on the trends
that are shaping our world.

Insight into trends.
Foresight for the future.
Confidence on
the path ahead.

Consulting@wired.co.uk